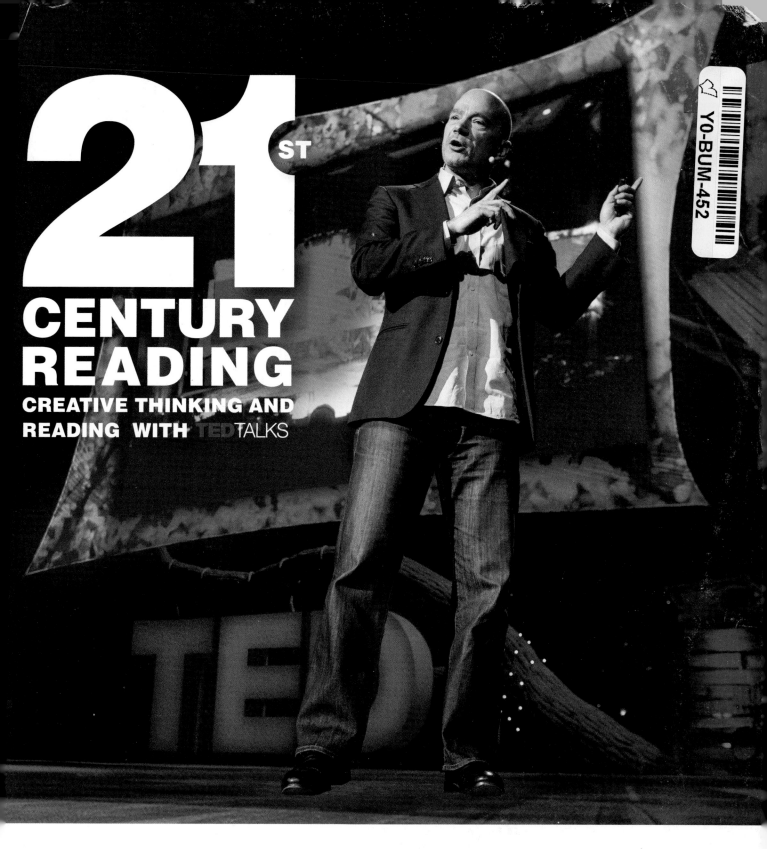

21ST CENTURY READING

CREATIVE THINKING AND READING WITH TED TALKS

Laurie Blass • Jessica Williams

NATIONAL GEOGRAPHIC LEARNING | CENGAGE Learning

Australia • Brazil • Japan • Korea • Mexico • Singapore • Spain • United Kingdom • United States

**21st Century Reading Student Book 4
Creative Thinking and Reading with
TED Talks**

Laurie Blass

Jessica Williams

Publisher: Andrew Robinson

Executive Editor: Sean Bermingham

Development Editors: Tom Jefferies and
    Christopher Street

Editorial Assistant: Dylan Mitchell

Director of Global Marketing: Ian Martin

Product Marketing Manager: Anders Bylund

Media Researcher: Leila Hishmeh

Director of Content and Media Production:
    Michael Burggren

Production Manager: Daisy Sosa

Senior Print Buyer: Mary Beth Hennebury

Cover and Interior Designers: Scott Baker
    and Aaron Opie

Cover Image: ©James Duncan Davidson/TED

Composition: Cenveo® Publisher Services

Student Book
ISBN 13: 978-1-305-26572-1

National Geographic Learning/Cengage Learning
20 Channel Center Street
Boston, MA 02210
USA

Cengage Learning is a leading provider of customised learning solutions with office locations around the globe, including Singapore, the United Kingdom, Australia, Mexico, Brazil and Japan. Locate our local office at **international.cengage.com/region**

Cengage Learning products are represented in Canada by Nelson Education Ltd.

Visit National Geographic Learning online at **NGL.Cengage.com**
Visit our corporate website at **www.cengage.com**

Printed in the United States of America
Print Number: 02   Print Year: 2016

CONTENTS

SCOPE AND SEQUENCE

Unit/Theme Academic field(s)	Lesson A	Reading	Reading Skills	Critical Thinking
1 WHY EXPLORE? *Science*		*The Urge to Explore* Magazine article	• Getting the main ideas • Identifying supporting information • Making inferences • Getting meaning from context	• Applying information
2 SUCCESS AND FAILURE *Education*		*A School in the Cloud* Blog interview	• Getting the main ideas • Finding supporting details • Recognizing point of view • Getting meaning from context	• Evaluating evidence • Reflecting on own experience
3 POWER SHIFTS *Business / Gender*		*Driving Change* Biographical article	• Getting the main ideas • Understanding key details • Interpreting statistics • Recognizing reference markers • Getting meaning from context	• Interpreting informatio
4 CREATIVE SPARKS *Media / Literature*		*Sparking Wonder and Possibility* Opinion article / Literary excerpts	• Getting the main ideas • Understanding a study • Analyzing literary excerpts • Getting meaning from context	• Interpreting research findings • Reflecting on own experience
5 HOPE AND EQUALITY *Sociology / Economics*		*Living on a Dollar a Day* Interview	• Getting the main ideas • Understanding key details • Paraphrasing Information • Getting meaning from context	• Interpreting meaning
6 BACKING UP HISTORY *Archaeology / Technology*		*Laser Preservation* Magazine article	• Getting the main ideas • Summarizing key details • Understanding a process • Getting meaning from context	• Reflecting on own experience
7 FOOD FOR ALL *Agriculture / Conservation*		*Feeding Nine Billion* Opinion essay	• Getting the main ideas • Identifying problems/solutions • Paraphrasing information • Understanding infographics • Getting meaning from context	• Evaluating recommendations
8 FUTURE JOBS *Business / Technology*		*Recipes for Innovation* Discursive article	• Understanding organization • Connecting purpose to main ideas • Understanding key details • Understanding a main message • Getting meaning from context	• Predicting future effect
9 HOW WE LEARN *Linguistics / Psychology*		*What Babies Know About Language and Why We Should Care* Scientific report	• Getting the main ideas • Understanding purpose/sequence • Applying information • Getting meaning from context	• Interpreting meaning
10 A BRIGHTER TOMORROW *Environment / Economics*		*Paths to the Future* Opinion essay	• Getting the main ideas • Understanding author's purpose • Understanding infographics • Getting meaning from context	• Inferring tone and attitude

Lesson B	TED Talks	Academic Skills	Critical Thinking	Project
	Why We Need the Explorers Brian Cox	• Previewing and predicting • Understanding key details • Understanding the main message	• Inferring purpose • Analyzing an argument • Reflecting on own experience	• Researching and presenting products
	How to Learn? From Mistakes Diana Laufenberg	• Previewing • Getting the main ideas • Integrating information • Analyzing an argument • Recognizing tone/attitude	• Predicting responses • Synthesizing information	• Writing a profile about someone who overcame failure
	Why We Have Too Few Women Leaders Sheryl Sandberg	• Previewing and predicting • Understanding main ideas and key details • Understanding purpose	• Evaluating an argument • Reflecting on own experience	• Researching women with successful careers
	The Mystery Box J.J. Abrams	• Predicting and previewing • Understanding key details • Analyzing problems and solutions	• Inferring reasons • Synthesizing information	• Creating a story to present
	The Good News on Poverty (Yes, There's Good News) Bono	• Previewing • Understanding main ideas • Understanding graphs • Identifying problems/solutions • Summarizing main ideas	• Analyzing graphical information • Analyzing causes • Evaluating methods	• Creating and presenting an infographic
	Ancient Wonders Captured in 3-D Ben Kacyra	• Previewing • Understanding key details • Identifying benefits • Understanding causes/effects	• Interpreting meaning • Applying information	• Recommending a historical site to preserve
	How Food Shapes our Cities Carolyn Steel	• Predicting • Understanding main and supporting ideas • Analyzing arguments	• Inferring purpose	• Presenting a proposal
	What Will Future Jobs Look Like? Andrew McAfee	• Previewing and predicting • Getting the main ideas • Identifying trends • Understanding solutions	• Predicting problems • Reflecting on own experience	• Creating a poster about future jobs
	The Linguistic Genius of Babies Patricia Kuhl	• Understanding main ideas • Understanding visuals • Recognizing a speaker's tone and message	• Interpreting meaning • Evaluating approaches • Synthesizing information	• Writing and sharing a blog
	Innovating to Zero! Bill Gates	• Predicting • Understanding main ideas and key details • Summarizing information	• Analyzing information • Interpreting a speaker's statement	• Presenting a report

WHAT IS 21ST CENTURY READING?

21ST CENTURY READING develops essential knowledge and skills for learners to succeed in today's global society. The series teaches core academic language skills and incorporates 21st century themes and skills such as global awareness, information literacy, and critical thinking.

Each unit of 21st Century Reading has three parts:

- **READ** about a 21st century topic—such as energy solutions—in Lesson A.
- **LEARN** more about the topic by viewing an authentic TED Talk in Lesson B.
- **EXPLORE** the topic further by completing a collaborative research project.

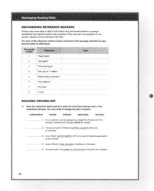

VOCABULARY BUILDING

READING SKILLS

LANGUAGE SKILLS

Strategies for understanding key ideas, language use, and purpose.

BUSINESS AND TECHNOLOGY

GLOBAL AWARENESS

21ST CENTURY THEMES

Interdisciplinary topics that affect everyone in a global society.

LEARNING SKILLS

The "4 Cs" that all learners need for success in a complex world.

CRITICAL THINKING AND COMMUNICATION

CREATIVITY AND COLLABORATION

21ST CENTURY LITERACIES

The ability to deal with information in a variety of modern formats and media.

VISUAL LITERACY

INFORMATION AND MEDIA LITERACIES

➔ For more on 21st century learning, see **www.p21.org/** and **21foundation.com/**

WHY EXPLORE?

An artist's impression of NASA's Mars Science Laboratory spacecraft approaching Mars. The Curiosity rover inside the spacecraft is now exploring Mars' surface.

GOALS

IN THIS UNIT, YOU WILL:

- Read about what motivates people to explore.
- Learn how exploration helps us understand our universe.
- Explore the practical value of scientific exploration.

THINK AND DISCUSS

1. At one time, vast areas of the Earth were unexplored. What do you think there is left to explore?

2. Where would you like to explore? Give reasons for your choice.

PRE-READING

A. Compare the photos on these pages and on pages 8-9. How is exploration similar now compared to the past? Discuss your ideas with a partner.

B. Read the title and introduction on this page, and the headings on pages 11–13. Note your answers to the questions below. Then discuss with a classmate.

1. The second heading in the passage is "Restless Genes." What does *restless* mean? What do you think *restless genes* means?

   _____

   _____

   _____

2. The final heading is "Exploring Beyond." Beyond what? What kind of exploration do you think this section will address?

   _____

   _____

   _____

3. The writer states that the urge to explore is a "defining part of human identity." What do you think this means?

   _____

   _____

   _____

THE URGE TO EXPLORE

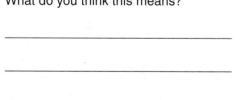 The compulsion to see what lies beyond that far ridge or that ocean— or this planet—is a defining part of human identity.

A sailing canoe in the waters close to the Truk Islands, Micronesia. The canoe is similar to those that the Polynesians used to explore the South Pacific hundreds of years ago.

THE AGE OF EXPLORATION

1 In the winter of 1769, the British explorer Captain James Cook received an astonishing gift from a Polynesian priest named Tupaia. It was a map, the first that any European had ever **encountered** that showed all the major islands of the South Pacific. Some accounts say Tupaia sketched the map on paper; others that he described it in words. What's certain is that this map instantly gave Cook a far more complete picture of the South Pacific than any other European possessed. It showed every major island group in an area some 3,000 miles across, from the Marquesas west to Fiji.

2 Cook had granted Tupaia a place on his ship, *Endeavour*, in Tahiti. Soon after that, the Polynesian impressed the crew by navigating to an island unknown to Cook. It was 300 miles south, but Tupaia never **consulted** a compass, chart, clock, or sextant. In the weeks that followed, as he helped guide the *Endeavour* from one archipelago to another, Tupaia amazed the sailors again and again. On request, at any time—day or night, cloudy or clear—he could point precisely toward Tahiti.

3 Cook, uniquely among European explorers, understood what Tupaia's feats meant. The islanders scattered across the South Pacific

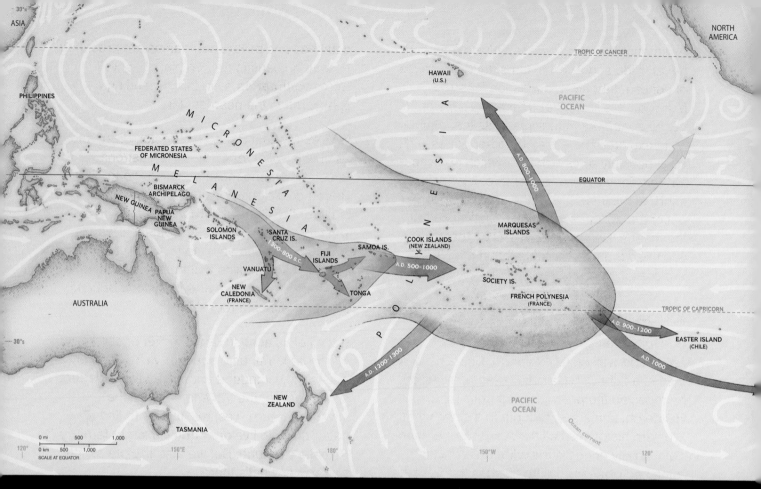

Polynesian pioneers: Some 3,000 years ago, a group of people known as the Lapita began traveling eastward from New Guinea, and within a few centuries reached Tonga and Samoa. A thousand years later, their Polynesian descendants pushed further, eventually even settling on the most remote islands of the Pacific.

were one people long ago who had explored, settled, and mapped this vast ocean without any of the navigational tools (except for boats) that Cook found essential—and they had carried the map **solely** in their heads ever since.

RESTLESS GENES

4 "No other mammal moves around like we do," says Svante Pääbo, a director of the Max Planck Institute for Evolutionary Anthropology in Leipzig, Germany. He uses genetics to study human origins. "There's a kind of madness to it. Sailing out into the ocean, you have no idea what's on the other side. And now we go to Mars. We never stop. Why?"

5 If an urge to explore rises in us **innately**, perhaps its foundation lies within our genome. In fact, there is a mutation that pops up

frequently in such discussions: a **variant** of a gene called DRD4. DRD4 helps control dopamine, a chemical messenger in the brain that plays a major role in reward-motivated behavior. Researchers have repeatedly tied the variant DRD4-7R—carried by roughly 20 percent of all humans—to increased curiosity and restlessness. Dozens of human studies have found that 7R makes people more likely to take risks; explore new places, ideas, foods, or relationships; and generally embrace movement, change, and adventure.

6 So is 7R the explorer's gene or adventure gene, as some call it? Yale University evolutionary and population geneticist Kenneth Kidd thinks that this overstates its role. Kidd speaks with special **authority** here, as he was part of the team that discovered the 7R variant 20 years ago. "You just can't reduce something as complex as human

exploration to a single gene." It would be better, Kidd suggests, to consider how groups of genes might lay a foundation for such behavior. It is likely that different groups of genes contribute to multiple traits that enable us to explore. There may be other genes—7R quite possibly among them—which go even further: They push us to explore. It helps, in short, to think not just of the urge to explore but of the ability—not just the motivation but the means. Before you can act on the urge, you need the tools or traits that make exploration possible.

EXPLORING BEYOND

7 Following the call of our restless genes has not ended well for all explorers. Captain Cook died in a fight with Hawaiians ten years after he received the precious map from Tupaia. His death, some say, brought to a close what Western historians call the Age of Exploration. Yet it hardly ended our exploring. We have remained **obsessed with** filling in the Earth's maps; reaching its farthest poles, highest peaks, and deepest trenches; sailing to its every corner and then flying off the planet entirely. With the NASA rover Curiosity now stirring us all as it explores Mars, some

countries and private companies are preparing to send humans to the red planet as well. Some **visionaries** even talk of sending a spacecraft to the nearest star.

8 NASA's Michael Barratt—a doctor, diver, and jet pilot; a sailor for 40 years; an astronaut for 12—is among those aching to go to Mars. Barratt consciously sees himself as an explorer like Cook and Tupaia. "We're doing what they did," he says. "It works this way at every point in human history. A society develops an enabling technology, whether it's the ability to preserve and carry food or build a ship or launch a rocket."

9 Not all of us ache to ride a rocket or sail the infinite sea. Yet, as a species, we're curious enough and intrigued enough by the **prospect** to help pay for the trip and cheer at the voyagers' return. Yes, we explore to find a better place to live or **acquire** a larger territory or make a fortune. But we also explore simply to discover what's there.

---

archipelago: *n.* a group of islands

feat: *n.* an act of skill, strength, or bravery

genome: *n.* all of the genes in an organism

mutation: *n.* a change in the genetic structure of an organism that makes it different

CHILD EXPLORERS

Alison Gopnik, a child-development psychologist at the University of California, Berkeley, says humans have a unique opportunity to develop the traits that encourage curiosity. We have a long childhood in which we can exercise our urge to explore while we're still dependent on our parents. While other animals play mainly by practicing basic skills such as fighting and hunting, Gopnik says that human children play by creating situations that test hypotheses. Can I build a tower of blocks as tall as me? What'll happen if we make the bike ramp go even higher?

During childhood, we develop the brain wiring and cognitive ability to explore effectively. As adults, this early practice allows us to take risks, test out possibilities, and shift strategies when necessary. Might there be a Northwest Passage? Could we get to the South Pole more easily on dogsleds? Maybe, just maybe, we could land a rover on Mars by lowering it from a hovercraft on a cable.

GETTING THE MAIN IDEAS

A. The reading passage is divided into three sections. Below, choose the sentence that best describes the main idea of each section.

Section 1: The Age of Exploration

a. Exploration began long before there were maps and other tools for navigation.

b. Captain Cook understood the powerful human urge to explore.

c. Both our urge and capacity to explore date back to the invention of boats.

Section 2: Restless Genes

a. Our genes are constantly changing, contributing to the human urge to explore.

b. There is an "exploration" gene called DRD4-R7.

c. Several different genes probably contribute to the human impulse to explore.

Section 3: Exploring Beyond

a. The human urge to explore can sometimes lead to disaster.

b. Much of our planet has been explored, but curiosity is pushing us to explore beyond Earth.

c. Technology is an essential element of exploration.

B. Which statement best describes the main idea for the whole reading passage?

a. We explore for many different reasons.

b. The compulsion to explore is an essential part of human identity.

c. The early Polynesians explored the islands of the Pacific.

IDENTIFYING SUPPORTING INFORMATION

A. Complete the chart with details (a–f) that support the main idea for each section of the passage.

a. Space programs like NASA are exploring Mars and other planets.

b. DRD4-7R may be responsible for the human urge to explore.

c. In 1769, Captain Cook received the first complete map of the South Pacific Islands.

d. Some people believe we should try to land a spacecraft on Earth's nearest star.

e. The impulse to explore helps explain the population patterns of the South Pacific Islands.

f. A specific mutation has been linked to exploration.

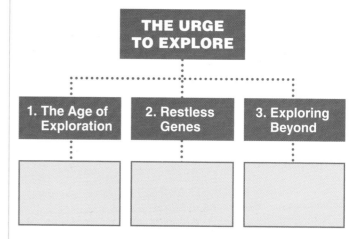

B. Geneticist Kenneth Kidd says that "Before you can act on the urge, you need the tools or traits that make exploration possible." Using the information in the "Child Explorers" section, answer the questions below with a classmate.

1. What abilities or traits do humans have that make them uniquely equipped to explore?

2. How are these traits developed in childhood?

3. In what ways could playing be connected to landing a rover on Mars?

MAKING INFERENCES

Sometimes writers do not say what they mean directly. Instead, they allow readers to draw their own conclusions. In other words, readers have to *make inferences* about what the writer means.

A. **What inferences can you make from these statements from the passage on pages 10–13? Choose a or b.**

1. "Tupaia amazed the sailors again and again. On request, at any time, day or night, cloudy or clear, he could point precisely toward Tahiti."

   a. They were amazed because of the tools he used in order to do this.

   b. They were amazed because they could not do what Tupaia could do.

2. DRD4 controls dopamine, a chemical messenger in the brain that plays a major role in reward-motivated behavior.

   a. Changes in dopamine levels cause some genes to mutate.

   b. The chemical dopamine may encourage people to take risks.

3. "Michael Barratt says, 'It works this way at every point in human history. A society develops an enabling technology, whether it's the ability to preserve and carry food or build a ship or launch a rocket.'"

   a. "Enabling technology" often makes new exploration possible.

   b. "Enabling technology" limits our exploration instincts.

B. **Compare your answers with a partner's. Explain how you arrived at the inference.**

A "selfie" of the Curiosity rover on the surface of Mars in 2013. The photo is a composite of dozens of images taken by a camera on its robot arm.

Developing Reading Skills

BUILDING VOCABULARY

A. Complete the paragraph with the words below.

consult   encountered   obsessed with   prospect   visionary

Captain James Cook was an 18th-century navigator and ___visionary___. He mapped
₁

many areas of the Pacific, New Zealand, and Australia, which at that time were unknown

territory to Europeans. The goal of Cook's first voyage was, in part, to search for the

legendary continent, Terra Australis. For years, members of the Royal Society had been

___dosessed with___ the idea of this continent, which was believed to exist far south in the
₂

Pacific Ocean, yet had never been seen. This unknown continent held the ___prospect___
₃

of great riches, so in 1769, the British government chose Cook as commander of *HMS*

Endeavour to search for Terra Australis. The *Endeavour* sailed to Tahiti, New Zealand,

and then along Australia's eastern coast, with Cook claiming all of the territory for Britain.

Cook never found Terra Australis, but during his voyages, he named and described

islands and other geographical features that he ___encountered___ and recorded his
₄

observations in his journal. This journal remains an important document that historians

continue to ___consult___ today.
₅

B. Review the words in bold in the passage on pages 11–13. Choose the word that is
closest to each word's meaning in the passage.

1. acquire

    a. receive   **b.** obtain   **c.** require   **d.** discover

2. authority

    a. understanding   **b.** force   **c.** emotion   **d.** expert knowledge

3. innately

    a. naturally   **b.** suddenly   **c.** gradually   **d.** without explanation

4. solely

    a. deliberately   **b.** completely   **c.** only   **d.** deeply

5. variant

    a. a different form   **b.** the only form   **c.** an earlier form   **d.** the most recent form

C. **Answer the questions below with a classmate.**

1. In the passage on page 16, Captain Cook was described as a **visionary**. Can you think of any other famous people who are visionaries?

2. Exploring is described in the passage as an **innate** ability of humans. What other human abilities do you think are innate?

GETTING MEANING FROM CONTEXT

Look at these sentences from the reading passage. Choose the phrase that is the closest in meaning to the phrases in bold.

1. "It would be better, Kidd suggests, to consider how groups of genes might **lay a foundation for** such behavior."

   a. give sufficient reason for something

   b. set the conditions that make something possible

2. "His death, some say, **brought to a close** what Western historians call the Age of Exploration."

   a. ended

   b. moved nearer

3. "Not all of us **ache** to ride a rocket or sail the infinite sea."

   a. want very badly

   b. are scared

4. "Yes, we explore to find a better place to live or acquire a larger territory or **make a fortune**."

   a. get lucky

   b. get rich

CRITICAL THINKING

Applying. Discuss the following questions with a partner.

a. What other explorers do you know of? Write a list below. Do you know what they discovered?

_____

_____

b. What do you think motivated these people to explore?

EXPLORE MORE

Search for more information about Captain Cook (pictured) and his explorations at nationalgeographic.com. Find out how these explorations changed our views of the world. Share your information with the class.

17

TEDTALKS

WHY WE NEED THE EXPLORERS

BRIAN COX Physicist, TED speaker

🔊 Although many historians believe that the Age of Exploration has passed, Brian Cox would likely disagree. He thinks that we're living through the greatest age of discovery and exploration our civilization has ever known.

Cox is a physicist who works at CERN's Large Hadron Collider in Switzerland, and is also a professor at Manchester University.

Cox may be best known in the United Kingdom as a public face of scientific research. He is the host of the BBC's *Big Bang Machine* and *Wonders of the Solar System*. Perhaps most importantly, he is a tireless champion of government funding for basic science and frequently urges the public to support scientific research. Government support for research, especially for basic science, is often reduced during economic downturns.

He urges all of us to continue reaching for the stars. Cox likes to quote the inventor Humphrey Davy, who said, "Nothing is so dangerous to the progress of the human mind than to assume that . . . there are no mysteries in nature, that our triumphs are complete, and that there are no new worlds to conquer."

---

champion: *n.* an enthusiastic supporter

funding: *n.* money provided by the government or by an organization for a special purpose

triumph: *n.* a victory; success

In this lesson, you are going to watch segments of Cox's TED talk. Use the information about Cox above to answer the questions on page 19.

Brian Cox's **idea worth spreading** is that we need to invest in curiosity-driven science because it fuels innovation and inspires a deeper understanding of our place in the universe.

1. Brian Cox has several professions. What are they?

   _____

2. How are they related?

   _____

3. Why do you think it might be "dangerous" to assume that our triumphs are complete?

   _____

PART 1

THE BEAUTY OF THE UNIVERSE

PREVIEWING

A. **Read this excerpt from Brian Cox's talk. Then discuss the questions below with a partner.**

❝ We live in difficult and challenging economic times, of course. And one of the first victims of difficult economic times, I think, is public spending of any kind, but [. . .] particularly curiosity-led science and exploration. So I want to try and convince you in about 15 minutes that that's a ridiculous and ludicrous thing to do. ❞

What do you think "curiosity-led science" means? Why do you think funding for curiosity-led science is cut during difficult economic times?

B. **Look at the photo of Enceladus below. What are the white things coming from the surface? Discuss your ideas with a partner.**

UNDERSTANDING KEY DETAILS

Now watch (▶) this segment from Cox's TED Talk, and answer the questions below with a partner.

1. What are the white things coming from the surface of Enceladus?

   a. clouds of dust   **b.** fountains of ice   **c.** beams of light

2. Why is this significant?

   _____

3. What makes the photograph of Earth on page 23 significant, according to Cox? Choose the two best answers.

   a. It was the first photograph taken from space.

   b. It made Earth appear small and fragile.

   c. It was shown on television.

   d. It shows a lot of the beautiful details of Earth's features.

   e. It raised awareness of the need to protect the environment.

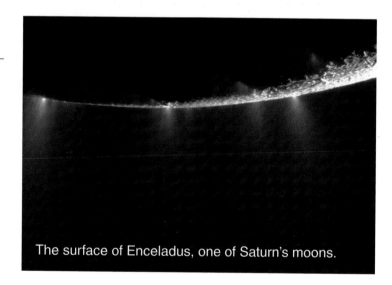

The surface of Enceladus, one of Saturn's moons.

CRITICAL THINKING

Inferring. Why do you think Cox chose these two specific photographs? What was his purpose for showing each one?

DRIVING INNOVATION

PREDICTING

Read this excerpt from the next segment of Brian Cox's talk.

❬❬ What's also not often said about the space exploration, about the Apollo program, is the economic contribution it made. ❭❭

What economic contributions do you think the exploration of the moon made? Discuss with a partner. Watch (▶) the next segment of his talk and check your ideas.

UNDERSTANDING KEY DETAILS

Read the summary of a scientific discovery Cox describes. Then complete the chart below with the steps (1–6) to show how one discovery led to other discoveries.

In the late 1800s, scientists made an astonishing discovery. When they heated up hydrogen atoms, the atoms gave off a strange light. Then the scientists discovered that each chemical element gives off its own unique patterns of different colored lights. This observation led to an understanding of basic atomic structure. This understanding, in turn, prompted the development of the quantum theory, which later led to an understanding of the behavior of electrons in one particular element, silicon, which, in turn, initiated the development of transistors.

---

atom: *n.* the smallest unit of any chemical element

quantum theory: the theory of the structure of atoms

silicon: *n.* a chemical used in many modern electronics

transistor: *n.* a small electronic part that controls the flow of electricity

1. Discovery that different elements emit different colors

2. Understanding of the behavior of electrons in silicon

3. Observation of patterns of light

4. Silicon used to make transistors—an essential part of modern electronics

5. Development of quantum theory

6. Understanding of the structure of atoms

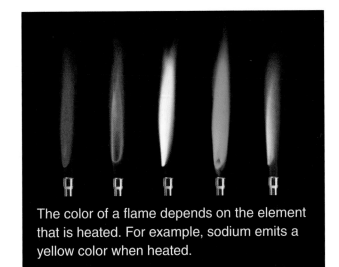

The color of a flame depends on the element that is heated. For example, sodium emits a yellow color when heated.

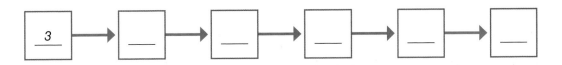

3 → → → → →

UNDERSTANDING THE MAIN MESSAGE

Use the information from Cox's talk to answer the questions below. Discuss your answers with a partner.

1. Why does Cox focus on space exploration and the discovery of atoms in his talk? Check (✔) the two best reasons.

   _____ **a.** They allow us to see the wonder of the universe.

   _____ **b.** They show how successful scientists are.

   _____ **c.** They have produced practical benefits.

2. What do you think Cox means when he says there is value in curiosity-based science?

   _____

   _____

CRITICAL THINKING

Analyzing. Read the excerpt below and answer the questions.

> « The argument has always been made, and it will always be made, that we know enough about the universe. You could have made it in the 1920s; you wouldn't have had penicillin. You could have made it in the 1890s; you wouldn't have the transistor. And it's made today in these difficult economic times: *Surely, we know enough. We don't need to discover anything else about our universe.* »

1. What point is Cox trying to make?

   a. The period between 1890 and today has been a time of great discovery.

   b. Continued exploration will lead to new, important discoveries.

   c. Difficult economic times are the best time for exploration.

2. What do you think? Has Cox persuaded you that cutting funding for science is "ridiculous"? Why, or why not? Discuss with a partner.

Reflecting. Cox suggests an important role for serendipity—the making of new discoveries by chance—in scientific research. Why does he think it is important?

EXPLORE MORE

Watch Cox's full TED Talk at TED.com. Where does he think we will find life in our solar system? Share what you learn with your class.

Project

This famous 1968 image, known as Earthrise, shows the Earth as seen from lunar orbit.

A. **Work with a partner. You are going to make a presentation to your class on some of the unanticipated benefits of one line of scientific curiosity—space exploration. Follow the steps below.**

1. With your partner, decide on the focus of your report. Choose one of the products or processes that has emerged as a result of space programs.

   - Artificial limbs
   - Ear thermometers
   - Fire fighting equipment
   - Freeze-drying
   - Memory foam for mattresses
   - Radial tires
   - Scratch-resistant lenses
   - Solar cells

2. Research your chosen product or process. Find out:

   - how and why it was first developed and used in the space program.
   - how it is used today outside of the space program.

3. Find a picture or video that illustrates how the product or process is used.

B. **Write up notes for your presentation. It should have three parts:**

   - Space program origins
   - Current use
   - Who has benefited most from this technology

C. **Present your findings to the class. Which product is the most useful?**

EXPLORE MORE

Learn more about current space explorations at news.nationalgeographic.com. Share your information with the class.

SUCCESS AND FAILURE

GOALS

IN THIS UNIT, YOU WILL:

- Read about the value of student-directed learning.
- Learn about the importance of making mistakes in education.
- Explore famous failures, and how some of them led to successes.

THINK AND DISCUSS

1. How do you think education today is different from 20 years ago? 50 years ago? 100 years ago?

2. Have you ever received a bad grade at school that you weren't expecting? Why do you think people sometimes get bad grades?

Sixth grade students use their iPad tablet computers during class at Pinnacle Peak Elementary School in Scottsdale, Arizona, U.S.A.

PRE-READING

A. Look at the photo and caption on pages 26–27. Who is the woman on the computer screen? What do you think she is doing? Discuss with a partner.

B. Read the introduction on pages 26–27. Then answer the questions below with a partner.

  1. What is the purpose of the School in the Cloud?

  _____

  _____

  _____

  2. What do you think are the advantages and disadvantages of the School in the Cloud?

  _____

  _____

  _____

  _____

C. Read the interview questions 1–6 on pages 27–28. Circle three topics (a–f) you think David Swancott will talk about. Check your ideas as you read the interview.

  a. why he retired

  b. why he decided to become a Skype Granny

  c. how students learn best

  d. a history of the School in the Cloud

  e. his experiences as a Skype Granny

  f. the differences between the British and Indian education systems

A SCHOOL IN THE CLOUD

POSTED BY NATASHA SCRIPTURE
TED Blog, October 14, 2014

The School in the Cloud—a project created by 2013 TED Prize winner Sugata Mitra—makes teachers available online to **mentor** children in schools around the world. As children explore the big questions that matter to them, they get nudges in the right direction from a Skype Granny. But

Granny = Abuelita
nudges = Empujones

A class at the Phaltan SOLE Lab in India interacts with a Skype Granny. Skype Grannies are teachers who use Skype to mentor children in self-organized learning classrooms around the world.

don't let the name fool you. While many Skype Granny participants are female and retired, just as many are male or in their 20s, 30s, and 40s. In the following interview, David Swancott, a retired biology teacher living in France, describes his experiences of being a Skype Granny over the last two years.

1. You're retired, living in the countryside. What inspired you to become a Skype Granny for School in the Cloud?

I found out about it on television—on the BBC's *The One Show*, which follows the evening news. They did a segment about the Granny Cloud, and it stirred my interest. I thought, "That's something I might like to be involved with." I missed being in contact with children. So I got in touch with the contact provided on the show's website, downloaded an application form, and, after an interview, I became a Skype Granny. Once a teacher, always a teacher.

2. **Every Tuesday morning, you Skype with young students at two different schools in India. Can you talk us through a typical session?**

Last week, one group came on and immediately wanted to know about butterflies. So, as time was tight, I quickly hunted out a National Geographic video on the monarch butterfly and we watched that. Afterwards, we talked through what they'd seen. I asked questions and together we explored the life cycle of a butterfly.

Sessions last between 30 and 45 minutes. We usually start by spending some time talking about the things that have happened during the week, then I show them some photos or a video or written material, usually on a topic they decided on the week before. We spend time talking about the material. I get them to give **input** as much as possible—picking out new vocabulary, checking spelling, and so on.

3. **You're the grandfather of two young boys and taught high school in England for more than 40 years, which means you must be very patient. What are some challenges you've come across being a Skype Granny?**

Well, you have to think on your feet a bit sometimes and be willing to move with the children if they go off on a tangent. Quite often, there are problems with sound or vision or even both, and we have to resort to communication by text. There's also no **guarantee** that the Internet will work at all, as the **facilities** in some areas are so poor. On one occasion, the line to the school was attacked by monkeys, and it took a while for it to be repaired, as the school is in a very remote area.

4. **What's the best thing about being a Skype Granny?**

The children's **enthusiasm**, their willingness to learn, and their appreciation of my involvement as a Granny. Recently, I've been experiencing some heart problems and when I restarted the sessions after my illness, the children at one of the schools had made these lovely "Get Well Soon" cards for me, which they were able to show to me during one of our sessions. What a tonic that was! And, unlike some of the children in England, when they see you, they smile. They are happy to be there. And they have a **contagious** enthusiasm, which I think is what keeps me going and makes me want to do more for them.

5. **What do you think makes a good teacher?**

Teaching is about creating and providing a supportive environment in which a child can learn. A good teacher acts as a facilitator for that child's learning. The U.K. government started fiddling around with education, and that's one of the things that drove me away from teaching—we moved to a very **prescribed** curriculum with little or no time to drift sideways and explore other facets of a subject or respond to students' questions or thoughts. The school's examination results became the most important thing, but it's much more than that! Overall, I think a good teacher must be able to work within the **constraints** of the existing system, have an enthusiasm for their subject, and be able to engage students and get them involved with their own learning.

6. **What do you think is the future of learning?**

The use of technology in schools is changing the way we learn, what we learn, and what the shape of the curriculum should be in the future. I was a teacher during an era when computers first appeared in schools—to be used by teachers, certainly not for students. Now, in many schools, the students all have their own computers or tablets. I never envisaged being able to communicate with a school in India on a regular basis, and now look what I am doing! Technology opens up many opportunities for different approaches to learning. Within this, children need to be allowed to take more charge of their learning, with the teacher acting in a more supporting role. **Letting go of** this control is a big challenge for teachers, as there is **security** when you are setting out the agenda. But really, this approach doesn't take anything away from the role of the teacher. We will continue to be instrumental in setting up these learning situations.

---

envisage: *v.* to imagine something that will happen in the future

tonic: *n.* something that makes you feel happy and full of energy

How Does the School in the Cloud Work?

Self-Organized Learning Environments (SOLEs) are created when educators encourage students to work as a community to answer their own questions by using the Internet.

1) Students are given a big question or are challenged to think of their own

2) Students choose their own groups and can change groups at any time

3) Students can move around freely, speak to each other and share ideas

4) Students can explore in any direction that they choose: there may be no single right answer

5) Groups are expected to present what they have learned at the end of the session

GETTING THE MAIN IDEAS

In interviews, the main ideas are introduced by the interviewer, so you can usually find them in the questions.

A. **Look at the interview questions from the passage on pages 26–29. Write the question number (1–6) for each of the main ideas (a–f) being introduced.**

_4_ **a.** some of the benefits of being a Skype Granny

_6_ **b.** how education will be different in the coming years

_1_ **c.** why Swancott started working as a Skype Granny

_3_ **d.** some of the difficulties Swancott has faced since becoming a Skype Granny

_2_ **e.** a description of an average Skype Granny class

_5_ **f.** the qualities of an effective instructor

B. **Review the interviewer's questions and David Swancott's responses. Then complete the sentences below that express the main ideas from the interview.**

Question 1: Swancott became a Skype Granny because he _____.

a. wanted to work with children again

b. interviewed for the job and thought he would like it

c. thinks children should be able to answer important questions

Question 2: His approach to teaching in the School in the Cloud is to _____.

a. use games to make lessons interesting

b. focus students on spelling and vocabulary

c. get students to actively participate in the class

Question 3: One of the challenges he has faced is that _____.

a. he loses patience

b. unexpected things happen

c. the children are not interested in the topic he chooses

Question 4: He thinks the best part of being a Skype Granny is that _____.

a. his students really appreciate his efforts

b. he can do all of his work on the Internet

c. his students remind him of his students in England

Question 5: He thinks a good teacher _____.

a. prepares students well for examinations

b. uses a prescribed curriculum

c. lets students explore and follow their interests

Question 6: One way education has changed is that _____.

a. there is greater use of technology

b. the teacher is not as important

c. there are fewer constraints on the curriculum

FINDING SUPPORTING DETAILS

For each main idea from Exercise A, find supporting details. Complete the outline below with the details.

1. Swancott was inspired to become a Skype Granny after _he SAW A SHOW ON the BBC's_.

2. Swancott's approach in a typical class is to

   start _TALKIN about things THAT HAVE HAPPENED during the week_

   include _photos or videos or written material_

   give students time _TO TALK ABOUT the material_.

3. Swancott's main challenge is _The main challenge is That The kids give opinion on everything_

4. One of Swancott's best experiences was _when he got A CARS from the children_.

5. Swancott thinks two characteristics of a good teacher are _a facilitator for that child's learning, and have an enthusiasm._

   _____.

6. One advantage of technology is that _opens up many opportunities for different approach to learning._

RECOGNIZING POINT OF VIEW

A. How would you describe Swancott's attitude toward the current approach to education in the U.K.? Is he critical or complimentary? Underline the parts of the passage that suggest his point of view.

B. Swancott gives his opinions about education today as well as what he thinks is a better approach. List three of his ideas for each category.

Swancott's view of current approaches to education	Swancott's ideas for a better approach to teaching
–	– Using the technology
–	– Students bring their computers and tablets
–	– Letting go of the control

BUILDING VOCABULARY

A. Circle the correct word or phrase to complete each sentence.

1. Decreases in education budgets place **constraints** / **guarantees** on resources for schools.

2. In some classrooms, students have a lot of **input** / **security** into how they learn.

3. Technology can help teachers **let go of** / **prescribe** the traditional approaches they used in the past.

4. Some teachers are **enthusiastic** / **contagious** about using new technology such as interactive whiteboards in their classrooms.

5. It is important for colleges to offer **facilities** / **mentors** for athletics and the performing arts.

B. Look at the information about Self-Organized Learning Environments on page 29. Use forms of the bolded words from Exercise A to complete the passage below.

The students in the School in the Cloud are participating in a new kind of education, called Self-Organized Learning Environments (SOLEs). In SOLEs, the teacher provides some sort of ___INPUT___, such as an interesting photograph, something from nature, or simply a big question. The students form groups and begin to find out about it.
They do not have the same ___CONSTRAINTS___ as they have in a traditional classroom.
For example, students are free to move around and follow their interests. They share information and control the discovery process. This kind of learning does not require high-tech ___FACILITIES___—just curiosity and an Internet connection. Of course, there is no ___GUARANTEES___ that children in SOLEs will learn more than students in traditional classrooms, but many students and their teachers are ___ENTHUSIASTIC___ about SOLEs.

C. Work with a partner to answer the questions below.

1. Have you ever had a **mentor**? How did he or she help you?
   NO

2. What kind of **facilities** do you think are most important for a university?

3. What **constraints** have you experienced in your educational system? Why do you think those constraints were/are there?

GETTING MEANING FROM CONTEXT

Find the bolded phrases below in the passage on pages 26–29. Then complete each sentence with the correct choice.

1. When someone **goes off on a tangent**, he or she _____. (Q. 3)

   a. starts talking about a different topic

   b. gets very angry

2. When you **resort to** something, it is _____. (Q. 3)

   a. the ideal option

   b. not your first choice

3. When people **think on their feet**, they _____. (Q. 3)

   a. talk and walk at the same time

   b. respond quickly

4. If you **take charge of** a project, you _____. (Q. 6)

   a. accept payment in return for work on it

   b. accept responsibility for it

CRITICAL THINKING

1. **Evaluating.** David Swancott believes he is making a difference in the lives of his students. What evidence does the passage provide for his belief?

2. **Personalizing.** Note your ideas for the questions below and discuss with a partner.

   a. How was your education similar to or different from the SOLE approach?

   b. What do you think is best—a "self-organized" education or a "prescribed curriculum"?

   c. Would you like to learn in a SOLE? Why, or why not?

EXPLORE MORE

Learn more about the School in the Cloud and Skype Grannies at http://www.theschoolinthecloud.org. In what other places is the School in the Cloud being used? Share what you learn with your classmates.

Students in Korakati, India, learn using the School in a Cloud web platform.

TEDTALKS

HOW TO LEARN?
FROM MISTAKES

DIANA LAUFENBERG, Educator, TED speaker

🔊 "I have not failed, I've just found 10,000 ways that won't work." These words from inventor Thomas Edison capture an idea that Diana Laufenberg thinks applies to education, too.

A teacher for more than a decade, Laufenberg has taught a variety of subjects to students of different ages and in a number of different cities. In all of these settings, she has shown a deep commitment to experiential learning, which takes "students from the classroom to the real world and back again."

She is also a passionate believer in developing resilience through experience, including making mistakes. She quotes educator John Dewey, who said, "The person who really thinks learns quite as much from his failures as from his successes." Today, Laufenberg travels all over the world helping other teachers develop their skills and expand their approaches to teaching. In particular, she encourages them to embrace project-based learning, in which teachers act as facilitators and allow students to direct their own learning.

---

embrace: *v.* to accept with enthusiasm

In this lesson, you are going to watch segments of Laufenberg's TED Talk.
Use the information about Laufenberg above to answer each question.

1. What might be an example of experiential learning?

   Zoom classes on an experiential learning now everybody is trying to learn online

2. Why do you think a teacher would want to take students "from the classroom to the real world and back again"?

   I think for the students learn in real situation and apply knoclese in real life

3. What do you think *resilience* means, and how is it related to learning from mistakes?

   for me means never stop trying even when you are failing because you only can get better when you know where diz you got wrong.

Diana Laufenberg's **idea worth spreading** is that students learn more when they can direct their own learning, connect lessons to real-life experiences, and embrace their failures.

TEDTALKS

GENERATIONS OF LEARNING

PREVIEWING

Read this excerpt from the beginning of Diana Laufenberg's talk. How is your education different from your grandparents' education?

> « In 1931, my grandmother [. . .] graduated from the eighth grade. She went to school to get the information because that's where the information lived. It was in the books; it was inside the teacher's head; and she needed to go there to get the information, because that's how you learned. »

GETTING THE MAIN IDEAS

A. Watch (▶) the first segment of Laufenberg's talk. Then complete the chart below to show the ways she and others in her family got access to information.

Laufenberg's grandmother and father	Laufenberg
go to school	_she had a library in the house_

B. Why was the encyclopedia significant for Laufenberg? Discuss your ideas with a partner.

INTEGRATING INFORMATION

A. What were Laufenberg's main reasons for joining the school in Philadelphia? Circle the two best answers.

1. The school gave teachers greater access to information.

2. The school did not have a traditional approach to teaching and learning.

3. The school shared Laufenberg's view on how kids learn.

4. The school showed Laufenberg how kids really learn when you leave them alone.

B. How were Laufenberg's goals related to the earlier discussion of her relatives? Note your ideas and discuss with a partner.

_____

_____

CRITICAL THINKING

Predicting. Read the excerpt below. How do you think Laufenberg will answer these questions? How would you answer them? Write some notes and then discuss with a partner.

❝ So, what do you do when the information is all around you? Why do you have kids come to school if they no longer have to come there to get the information? **❞**

PART 2

LEARNING FROM MISTAKES

ANALYZING AN ARGUMENT

A. **In the next segment of her talk, Laufenberg describes a project her students did. Read the summary below. Then watch (▶) the next segment of the talk, and answer the questions.**

Laufenberg's students were asked to produce infographics about man-made disasters. They were a little uncomfortable with this because they had never prepared infographics before. But Laufenberg told the students, "Go figure it out." When they finished, the students evaluated their infographics and found some were not that great. They discussed what worked and what they had learned. Laufenberg thinks her students will do better next time because of this learning process.

1. Was Laufenberg expecting her students to produce perfect infographics? Why, or why not?

   No because she know they going to make mistakgs.

2. What did she want them to learn?

   She want to learn from her mistakes, so they can do better the next time.

3. In what way did the infographic project represent a failure?

   their wasn't enough information and it

4. Why does Laufenberg think failure is an important part of learning?

   because when you fail you know what you did wrong and next time you'll making correct, you'll not do the same mistake

B. **Do you think this story is an effective example for Laufenberg's argument? Why, or why not? Discuss with a partner.**

RECOGNIZING TONE AND ATTITUDE

A. **Laufenberg includes categorical statements and words that show how important and urgent the issue is to her. Look at the excerpt below and notice the underlined phrases. Then circle the best paraphrase of her main point.**

❝ We deal right now in the educational landscape with an infatuation with the culture of one right answer that can be properly bubbled on the average multiple-choice test, and I am here to share with you: It is not learning. ❞

1. Sometimes it could be a mistake to think learning is just about getting right answers on a test.

2. Today, it is wrong for educators to be obsessed with the idea that learning is only about getting right answers on a test.

B. **Read the excerpt below and answer the questions with a partner.**

❝ The main point is that, if we continue to look at education as if it's about coming to school to get the information and not about experiential learning, empowering student voice, and embracing failure, we're missing the mark. And everything that everybody is talking about today isn't possible if we keep having an educational system that does not value these qualities, because we won't get there with a standardized test, and we won't get there with a culture of one right answer. We know how to do this better, and it's time to do better. ❞

1. How would you describe Laufenberg's attitude toward current education policies? Is it positive, neutral, or critical? *Critical*

2. Underline the words that signal this attitude.

3. What three qualities does she think an educational system should have?
   coming to school to get the information and not about experiential learning   *empowering student voice*   *embracing failure*

CRITICAL THINKING

Synthesizing. Discuss the following questions with a partner.

1. Review questions 5 and 6 from page 28. How would you answer these questions?

2. How do you think Laufenberg would answer these questions?

3. In what ways do Laufenberg and Swancott share the same perspectives?

EXPLORE MORE

Watch Diana Laufenberg's full TED Talk at TED.com. Discover more of her ideas about the importance of exploration and failure for students.

Project

The rapper Jay Z performs at a concert. Despite not being able to get a record deal in the 1990s, Jay Z eventually became one of the best-selling hip-hop artists of all time.

A. **Work on your own or with a partner. Write a profile of someone who experienced significant failure at first but went on to succeed. Pick a famous person from the list below or someone you know.**

Walt Disney	Thomas Edison	Henry Ford	Soichiro Honda
Jay Z	Steve Jobs	Michael Jordan	Akio Morita
J.K. Rowling	Dr. Seuss	Steven Spielberg	Vera Wang

B. **Research the following:**

- What was the person trying to do or create?
- Why did it fail?
- According to this person, what did he or she learn from the experience of failure?
- How did he or she succeed in the end?
- How do/will we remember him or her?

C. **Present your report to your classmates. Include images of the person in your report and other visuals that will make your report more interesting.**

EXPLORE MORE

Learn more about famous failures in history—and the people who learned from them—by reading the article at ngm.nationalgeographic.com/2013/09/famous-failures. Share what you learned with the class.

Truck operator Carrie Simms at the Albian Sands
Mine in Fort McMurray, Canada

POWER
SHIFTS

IN THIS UNIT, YOU WILL:

- Read about someone who is challenging traditional gender roles.
- Learn how some women make choices about career and family.
- Explore the careers of other women leaders.

THINK AND DISCUSS

1. What kinds of skills or qualities do you think are needed to become a leader in business? Give some examples.

2. Are there any jobs that are more likely to be filled by men than by women? Are there any jobs that are typically done by women? Give some examples.

PRE-READING

A. Look at the photo and the introduction to the passage. Write notes for each question below, and then discuss your ideas with a partner.

1. Why do you think rickshaw driving has been a male-dominated job?

   because most of the contry think women have to stay home and the men have ~~to provide~~

2. Why do you think Avani Singh is trying to change that?

   She want help women get some empowerment

3. What steps do you think she can take to change it?

   recruit more women that has the same thoust that she has

B. Study the graph on page 45. Discuss the questions with a partner.

1. What percentage of women participate in the workforce in India?

   _50%_

2. How does this compare to other countries?

   They are most the same

C. Read the heading and first sentence of each section in the passage. How do you think the workforce is changing in India? Discuss with a partner.

DRIVING CHANGE

Among the cars, trucks, and cows of Delhi's busy streets, bicycle rickshaws— three-wheeled people-carriers—zip through the traffic. Rickshaw driving has been a traditionally male-dominated profession. However, 17-year-old Avani Singh is trying to change that.

In India's biggest cities, such as New Delhi and Kolkata, rickshaws are often the fastest and cheapest way to get around.

A CHANGING WORKFORCE?

1 Singh is part of a new generation of Indian women. More and more women in India— about 30 percent—are working outside of the home. Women also make up more than 40 percent of the student population in the country, and that figure is growing. Many are choosing traditionally male-dominated careers in engineering and technology, although their representation in these fields remains small.

2 The situation in India **mirrors** global trends. Worldwide, an average of 50 percent of all women participate in the workforce, but behind this figure there are some hard facts. In 2012, about half of these women were working in service jobs, just over a third were working in agriculture, and only about 16 percent had jobs in industry and technology. This last figure has not changed in 20 years.

◀ Kohinoor, Delhi's first female driver of an electric rickshaw

3 Working women face very real challenges as they try to strike a balance between their careers and family life. Around the world, women are often expected to make sure that life at home runs smoothly: that meals are prepared, that the family has clean clothes, and that the house is tidy. In reality, they have two, often full-time, jobs. It's tough, but in spite of this, many say they appreciate the independence and income their careers provide; they also value their roles as wives and mothers, however.

A SENSE OF EMPOWERMENT

4 Avani Singh wanted to help women in the slums of Delhi feel a sense of empowerment. Growing up in New Delhi, her route to school took her past the city's slums. In this city of 17 million, these areas of poverty stretch for miles. To Singh, they seemed just a part of the city—always there, unchanging. But as she grew older, it began to dawn on her: Not everyone had what she had. And she could help.

5 The idea first came to her when she learned about a new kind of bicycle rickshaw. Bright green and futuristic, it was electric-powered, thanks to a solar panel on the roof. The electric motor made it easier to pedal. Singh, then only 16 years old, had an insight: Rickshaw driving—traditionally a job for men because of its physical demands—could now be a job for women, too.

6 In 2012, Singh **founded** Ummeed ki Rickshaw, a program that trains women from the slums of Delhi to become rickshaw drivers. Through this initiative, she gives women a way to earn both a living and a level of social mobility that were previously unimaginable—all before she's old enough to get a driver's license of her own.

7 Singh started Ummeed ki Rickshaw with a single electric rickshaw, **donated** by a local manufacturer. Then she needed to find a driver, so in **collaboration** with the Delhi-based non-governmental organization Centre for Equity and Inclusion, she put out a call for **volunteers** in Jamia, a slum near her home. "When I first advertised the program, 15 women came to hear about it," she remembers. "They were bubbling with energy and were so excited by the idea." The first rickshaw went to Kohinoor, a 33-year-old single mother of two. Kohinoor's father died when she was four years old, and she started working when she was just eight. After years of struggle, she became Delhi's first female electric rickshaw driver.

ECONOMIC MOBILITY

8 In a city where female drivers are rare, *Ummeed*, which means "hope" in Hindi, is carving out a space for female economic mobility. The program gives women an opportunity for economic independence. Singh even earned the attention of India's

Minister of New and Renewable Energy, Farooq Abdullah, who **endorsed** the program because electric rickshaws are environmentally friendly.

9 Many of the young girls that Singh works with get married before they've ever left their village—half of them by age 13. They don't understand that they can be wives and mothers and also have good jobs. Ummeed ki Rickshaw helps them to realize their potential and **aspire** to do something to create better lives for themselves and their families. Singh explains, "Ummeed ki Rickshaw is a really small step—it's practically nothing if you look at it from the country's perspective or from the world's perspective. But I think something small like this can help inspire a young generation to make a difference."

10 Singh's partners at the Center for Equality and Inclusion are confident that the rickshaw project will help women balance their new freedoms with the traditional roles they have to **fulfill** at home. Says one spokesperson, "This has provided our women an exciting opportunity to break **stereotypes** and **take on** new challenges."

---

slum: *n.* a poor and usually crowded part of a city

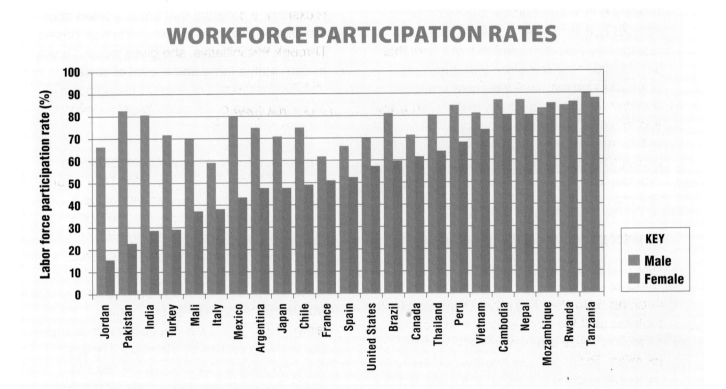

WORKFORCE PARTICIPATION RATES

Source: ILO, EAPEP, 6th edition

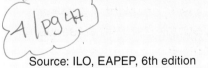

▲ Worldwide, there are far fewer women participating in the workforce than men—though the percentage rates vary widely from country to country. In India, less than 30 percent of women who are able to work outside the home are actually employed, compared to over 80 percent of men.

A worker assembles a motorcycle at a factory near Caracas, Venezuela.

GETTING THE MAIN IDEAS

Complete the summary of the passage with three of the statements below.

Globally, women are participating in the workforce in greater numbers than ever before. However, there is a downside: _5_. One reason for this is that women are often expected to fulfill their roles as homemakers. In spite of these challenges, _4_. In India, Avani Singh is helping women increase their participation in the workforce by opening up job opportunities in transportation. These jobs can increase their economic mobility and independence, and _2_.

1. even young people can make a difference by creating innovative solutions to problems

2. this can bring women a sense of empowerment

3. India remains a very traditional country with clear limits to what certain people can do

4. many women manage to hold jobs outside the home at the same time that they maintain traditional cultural roles

5. women's participation in the workforce is in a relatively narrow range of jobs

E

UNDERSTANDING KEY DETAILS

Complete the concept map about Ummeed ki Rickshaw.

Founded by a ___16___ –year-old student named _Avani Singh_

Endorsed by India's Minister for New and Renewable Energy because the program is _envairomently friendly_.

Gives women an opportunity to gain _economy_ independence.

Goal is to train _women_ to be rickshaw drivers.

Ummeed ki Rickshaw

First participant was a _single_ mother named Kohinoor.

Ummeed means _Hope_ in Hindi.

INTERPRETING STATISTICS

Use information from paragraphs 1 and 2 on page 43 and the graph on page 45 to answer the questions.

1. Approximately what percentage of women in the global workforce are employed in the service industry?

   30% percent

2. In the last 20 years, has the percentage of women in industry and technology jobs gone up, gone down, or stayed the same?

   stay the same

3. Name two countries where women's participation in the workforce is above 70 percent.

   Nepal, Tanzania.

4. In what countries is the level of participation in the workforce by men and women the closest? In what countries is the difference in workforce participation between the sexes the greatest?

   JORDAN, PALISTAN, india AND TU

5. Why do you think the percentage of women in the workforce varies from country to country?

   Differents cultures

RECOGNIZING REFERENCE MARKERS

Writers have many ways to refer to information they mentioned earlier in a passage. Sometimes they repeat a word or use a pronoun. They may also use synonyms or use general category words that include the idea.

For each of the reference markers below, look back at the passage and find the topic that the writer is referring to.

Paragraph	Reference	Topic
1	"these fields"	Engeneering and tecnology.
2	"this figure"	the women's portent. 50% (workforce)
2	"This last figure" →shape or number	the women's porcent workn on Industrys. 16%
4	"this city of 17 million"	New Delhi
4	"these areas of poverty"	City's slums
6	"this initiative"	Rickshaw
7	"the idea"	to find other drivers
8	"a city"	New Delhi

BUILDING VOCABULARY

A. **Read the sentences below and then write the word that matches each of the underlined phrases. You may need to change the part of speech.**

collaboration   donate   endorse   stereotype   volunteer

stereotype **1.** It is a <u>common, but not always true, idea</u> that physical jobs like driving a rickshaw are not appropriate for women.

endorse **2.** The government of India has <u>publicly supported</u> the work of Ummeed.

collaboration **3.** Avani Singh <u>worked together</u> with a non-governmental organization on her project.

donate **4.** Green Wheels <u>freely provided</u> a rickshaw to Ummeed.

Volunteers **5.** Ummeed asked for <u>people to come forward</u> to try the new rickshaw.

B. Choose the word or phrase that is closest in meaning to the word in bold as it is used in the article.

1. **mirrors** (Paragraph 2)

   is clear   is similar to   proves   contrasts with

2. **founded** (Paragraph 6)

   claimed   located   established   discovered

3. **aspire** (Paragraph 9)

   hope   look for   work hard   deserve

4. **fulfill** (Paragraph 10)

   accept   perform   respect   consider

5. **take on** (Paragraph 10)

   bring   accept   answer   create

C. Discuss the following questions with a partner.

1. Have you ever **collaborated** on a project? Describe how the collaboration worked.

2. What other kinds of **stereotypes** do you know of? Describe them.

GETTING MEANING FROM CONTEXT

Find these phrases in the passage and then match them with their definitions.
There are two definitions that are not needed.

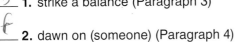

___b__ 1. strike a balance (Paragraph 3)

___f__ 2. dawn on (someone) (Paragraph 4)

___c__ 3. earn a living (Paragraph 6)

___g__ 4. social mobility (Paragraph 6)

___d__ 5. realize one's potential (Paragraph 9)

a. as a result of

b. to give appropriate attention to two or more different ideas

c. to make enough money to buy what you need

d. to achieve as much as is possible

e. to hit something in the right way

f. to begin to understand something

g. movement to a higher level of society

CRITICAL THINKING

Interpreting. Read paragraph 2 again and discuss the following questions with a partner.

1. What are the "hard facts" that the author refers to?

2. What do you think is the significance of these facts?

EXPLORE MORE

Learn more about projects to empower women in India at cequinindia.org. Share what you learn with the rest of the class.

TEDTALKS

WHY WE HAVE TOO FEW WOMEN LEADERS

SHERYL SANDBERG Business executive, TED speaker

"In my generation, there will not be 50 percent of [women] at the top of any industry," says Sheryl Sandberg, Chief Operating Officer of Facebook, the world's largest social networking site.

Sandberg manages Facebook's sales, marketing, and communications. Before working at Facebook, Sandberg managed Google's online sales operation, and before that, she served as an economist for the World Bank. Today, she is one of few women at the "C" level of a large company—that is, Chief Executive Officer, Chief Operating Officer, Chief Financial Officer, etc.

Sandberg urges each woman to make the choices that work best for her family and her career. However, she is concerned that women who choose to pursue an active career are not sufficiently confident and assertive, and that companies do not appropriately recognize those who are. In general, she says that women have not advanced in leadership roles as much as she would like. But she is hopeful about a future in which more women are leaders. She thinks that a world where half of our companies were run by women "would be a better world."

---

assertive: *adj.* behaving in a confident way

Sheryl Sandberg's **idea worth spreading** is that women who want to advance their careers and raise a family need to share equal responsibility with their spouses, be confident in the workplace, and seek out new opportunities at work.

In this lesson, you are going to watch segments of Sandberg's TED Talk. Use the information about Sandberg on page 50 to answer each question.

1. What did Sandberg do before working at Facebook?

   As an economist for the World Bank.

2. What are Sandberg's main concerns about women in the workforce?

   That women are not sufficiently confident and assertive.

3. Do you agree with Sandberg's opinion that the world would be a better place if more women ran companies? Explain your answer.

   Yes, because in this way maybe more equality we women will have

TEDTALKS

PROBLEMS AT THE TOP

PREVIEWING AND PREDICTING

[handwritten: 15/16% women at the top? 20%]
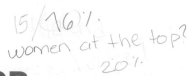

A. **Read this excerpt from Sheryl Sandberg's talk and answer the questions below.**

❝ So for any of us in this room today, let's start out by admitting we're lucky. We don't live in the world our mothers lived in, our grandmothers lived in, where career choices for women were so limited. And if you're in this room today, most of us grew up in a world where we had basic civil rights, and amazingly, we still live in a world where some women don't have them.

But all that aside, we still have a problem, and it's a real problem. And the problem is this: Women are not making it to the top of any profession anywhere in the world. The numbers tell the story quite clearly. A hundred and ninety heads of state—nine are women. Of all the people in parliament in the world, 13 percent are women. In the corporate sector, women at the top, [. . .] tops out at 15, 16 percent. The numbers have not moved since 2002 and are going in the wrong direction. [. . .] We also have another problem. . . . »

[handwritten left margin: sit in the ??? Parrot don't live before you ???]

civil rights: *n.* equal protection and treatment by law

corporate sector: *n.* private companies

heads of state: *n.* leaders of countries

1. What kind of jobs is she focusing on? *heads of states*

2. Do any of the figures she provides surprise you? Explain why or why not.

No, she retnats very well what happens in the world men has more opportunities and have a better payment and women not.

B. **Work with a partner. Make some notes and then discuss the questions. Then check your ideas as you watch (▶) the first part of the talk.**

1. Why do you think the number of women in top positions in business is not moving, or going in the "wrong" direction?

_____

_____

2. What "other problem" do you think Sandberg will discuss in the rest of her talk?

_____

_____

GETTING THE MAIN IDEAS

What "other problem" does Sandberg name? Check (✓) one of the three options below.

✓ 1. Women are not making it to the top of their professions because they often do not want to compete with men.

_____ 2. Unlike men, professional women are often forced to choose between pursuing their career and having a family.

_____ 3. We are not giving clear messages to our daughters about succeeding in the workplace.

PART 2

A SEAT AT THE TABLE

PREVIEWING

In her full TED Talk, Sandberg goes on to outline three ways women can stay in the workforce. Read two of her suggestions below. Then discuss the questions with a partner.

❝ Don't leave before you leave. Stay in. Keep your foot on the gas pedal until the very day you need to leave to take a break for a child—and then make your decisions. Don't make decisions too far in advance, particularly ones you're not even conscious you're making. ❞

❝ [M]ake your partner a real partner. [. . .] If a woman and a man work full time and have a child, the woman does twice the amount of housework the man does, and the woman does three times the amount of childcare the man does. So she's got three jobs or two jobs, and he's got one. Who do you think drops out when someone needs to be home more? ❞

1. What do you think Sandberg means when she tells women, "Don't leave before you leave"?

2. What do you think she means by "Make your partner a real partner"?

UNDERSTANDING MAIN IDEAS

Watch (▶) the next segment of Sandberg's talk where she explains her third point. Then answer the questions below.

1. What does she mean when she says women should "sit at the table"? Choose the two best statements.

   a. Women should be vocal about their abilities.

   b. Women should be active participants at work.

   c. Women should not take time off from work.

2. Why does Sandberg think women don't always "sit at the table"? Choose the best reason.

   a. Men attribute their success to themselves, and women attribute it to external factors.

   b. Those in management positions are less likely to recognize women's achievements than men's.

UNDERSTANDING KEY DETAILS

A. **Read the summary of one of the stories Sandberg tells. What similarities and differences did the students see between "Heidi" and "Howard"? Complete the Venn diagram with the information (a–e).**

Harvard Business School wrote a report about a very successful CEO named Heidi Roizen. A professor at Columbia University did an experiment using that report with two groups of students. He told one group that the information was about a woman named Heidi Roizen. He told the other group that the information was about a man named Howard Roizen. That one-word change made a really big difference.

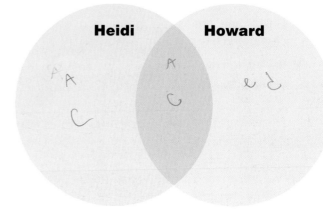

a. competent   **d.** not good to work with

b. good to work with   **e.** political

c. likeable

B. **Sandberg says to women: "Believe in yourself and negotiate for yourself." How does the "Heidi story" illustrate her point? Discuss with a partner.**

UNDERSTANDING PURPOSE

Sandberg tells a story about a colleague who came to see her after a meeting. Answer the questions below with a classmate.

1. What did her colleague notice about the men in the meeting?

2. What point was Sandberg's colleague trying to make?

3. Why do you think Sandberg included this story in her talk?

CRITICAL THINKING

1. Evaluating. Do you think that most working women would be able to follow Sandberg's three pieces of advice? Explain why or why not, giving some examples.

2. Reflecting. Have you or has anyone you know had to make this choice between career and family? It could be a man or a woman. Describe the situation to a partner.

EXPLORE MORE

Watch Sheryl Sandberg's full talk at TED.com. Find out more about the two other ways Sandberg suggests that women can stay in the workforce. Report back on what you learned to your class.

Project

Margaret Chan, Director-General of the World Health Organization

A. Work with a partner. You are going to research women who have reached the top of their profession. Choose one of the women below, or find one on your own.

Michelle Bachelet
Arundhati Bhattacharya
Ursula Burns
Margaret Chan
Park Geun-hye
Ellen Johnson Sirleaf
Christine Lagarde

Marissa Mayer
Angela Merkel
Indra Nooyi
Irene Rosenfeld
Dilma Rousseff
Meg Whitman
Oprah Winfrey

B. Use the prompts below to guide your research.

- Background: where she grew up/her education
- Career development: how she reached a leadership position
- Current position
- Family life: Does she have children? Other significant responsibilities or interests?

C. Present your findings to your classmates. Your report should have three parts:

1. Background and development of the woman's career
2. Current position and recent accomplishments
3. Career/family balance

EXPLORE MORE

Check out the TED Talk playlist "10 talks by women that everyone should watch" at TED.com. Share what you learn with the class.

CREATIVE
SPARKS

In a scene from J.J. Abrams's *Star Trek*, crew members of the Starship Enterprise race to prevent an alien drilling platform from destroying the planet Vulcan. In his TED Talk, Abrams reveals how good storytelling keeps viewers engaged by constantly making them guess what's going to happen next. As Abrams says in his talk, "There are times when mystery is more important than knowledge."

GOALS

IN THIS UNIT, YOU WILL:

- Read about stories that stimulate the imagination.
- Learn how movie director J.J. Abrams finds his inspiration.
- Explore ways to create stories using technology.

THINK AND DISCUSS

1. Look at the photo. What type of movie is *Star Trek*? Why do you think movies like this are popular?

2. What do you think makes a good story? Give examples of books, TV shows, or movies that tell a good story.

Lesson A

PRE-READING

A. Read the introduction and first paragraph of the passage. Write down some notes for the following questions. Then discuss your ideas with a partner.

1. Who do you think the "app generation" is? What age group might they belong to?

   Kids born in work of
   Tecnologis 2000 until now

2. The author says that this generation prefers narrative realism when they write. What do you think this kind of writing is? Why do teenagers like writing in this way?

   because most of the time
   we write about un experiency 'so
   And include on imaginato and I
   think kids now are stuck with
   tecnoly and confusini about the
   feeling

B. Look at the book covers on page 61 and answer the questions. Then discuss your ideas with a partner.

1. What do you think the two stories are about?

   imagination and
   mystery

2. What might the two stories have in common?

   A parralalel world a
   fiction story

3. Have you ever read anything like these stories?

   Yes.

In his artwork for *The Martian Chronicles*, a short story collection by writer Ray Bradbury, illustrator Michael Whelan portrays an imaginary alien landscape.

Many members of the so-called "app generation" struggle with creative writing—as a new study suggests, they're turning into realists.

1 Creative writing is part of being a kid. Writing and reading wild stories of lost kingdoms and Mars colonies help the imagination grow strong. But a recent study uncovers an interesting, perhaps even dismaying, trend: This generation of kids seems to prefer narrative realism when they write.

SPARKING WONDER AND POSSIBILITY

BY **LAURA McCLURE** Adapted from her TED Blog, June 6, 2014

2   In a study published in *Creativity Research Journal*, researchers at the Harvard Graduate School of Education and the University of Washington asked the question, "How have the style, content, and form of adolescents' art-making and creative writing changed over the last 20 years?"

3   To answer that question, researcher Emily Weinstein examined traditional hallmarks of creativity, such as originality, complexity, and sophistication, in two **distinct** eras of teenage self-expression. After **analyzing** 354 visual artworks and 50 fiction stories from two separate time periods (1990–1995 and 2006–2011), there's good and bad news.

4   The good news? Adolescent visual **proficiency** has improved. The bad news: Teen creativity and technical skill in writing has declined. Instead of imagining Martian neighborhoods, the app generation has been describing their own summer plans.

Why is this happening? From the study:

5 "The observed domain changes could undeniably be the result of any number of **societal** changes over the period of interest. Two changes **highlighted** by Kim (2011), however, may be particularly relevant to high school students' experiences and their creative expression: the increase in digital media technologies and the rise of standardized testing in schools."

6 This is a small study, but if it inspires you to think about how to develop the imaginations of the kids and teens you know, may we suggest this **option**: Read and share fiction that sparks wonder and possibility. And to this writer, that means **genre** fiction: science fiction and fantasy that pulls you out of narrative realism and into a world of possibility. If you already love science fiction and fantasy, I encourage you to plant seeds of inspiration by sharing your favorite authors with a teenager or young person you like. (And if you don't think you like genre fiction, the authors excerpted here may change your mind.)

7 There's **obviously** plenty more where these came from! More personal favorites: Neil Gaiman, Terry Pratchett, Patrick Rothfuss, Neal Stephenson, Philip K. Dick, David Wong, John Scalzi, Ernest Cline, William Gibson, and Madeleine L'Engle.

8 Now it's your turn. Who are your beloved science fiction and fantasy authors?

---

dismaying: *adj.* discouraging

narrative realism: *n.* literature that describes things in a realistic way

spark: *v.* to cause an action or a result

A store owner takes a break from reality at an open-air bookstore in Skopje, Macedonia.

STORIES WORTH SHARING

Here are excerpts from two imaginative stories that might inspire some wild thinking.

The Veldt, by Ray Bradbury

Why you'd want to give this to a teen: Bradbury is a reliable source of creative inspiration; this story is a classic introduction to his work.

Excerpt: "The nursery was silent. It was empty as a jungle glade at hot high noon. The walls were blank and two-dimensional. Now, as George and Lydia Hadley stood in the center of the room, the walls began to purr and recede into crystalline distance, it seemed, and presently an African veldt appeared, in three **dimensions**, on all sides, in color reproduced to the final pebble and bit of straw. The ceiling above them became a deep sky with a hot yellow sun."

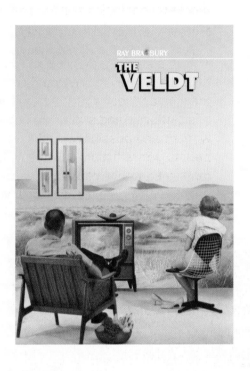

---

glade: *n.* an open space in the woods or forest

crystalline: *adj.* very clear

veldt: *n.* a large, flat area where mainly grass grows, especially in South Africa

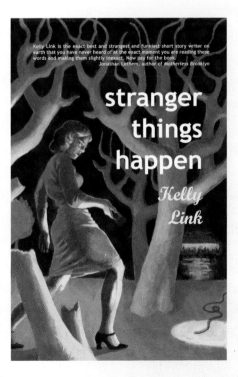

The Specialist's Hat, by Kelly Link

Why you'd want to give this to a teen: Everyone loves a good scary story, right? This one definitely fits the bill. Warning: Not bedtime reading, at any age.

Excerpt: "'When you're Dead,' Samantha says, 'you don't have to brush your teeth.' 'When you're Dead,' Claire says, 'you live in a box, and it's always dark, but you're not ever afraid.' Claire and Samantha are **identical** twins. Their combined age is twenty years, four months, and six days. Claire is better at being Dead than Samantha. The babysitter yawns, covering up her mouth with a long white hand. 'I said to brush your teeth and that it's time for bed,' she says. She sits cross-legged on the flowered bedspread between them."

The Specialist's Hat is a short story that appears in Link's book *Stranger Things Happen*.

GETTING THE MAIN IDEAS

Use information from pages 58–60 to answer the questions.

1. What did the researchers conclude?

    a. Teens no longer write realistically, but have improved their ability to write creatively.

    b. Digital media technologies have improved adolescents' visual skills as well as their ability to write creatively.

    c. Teens' writing skills are not as good as they used to be, and their writing tends to be less creative than it was before.

2. What did the survey results suggest to Laura McClure?

    a. Having teens read science fiction and fantasy novels is a good way to develop their imaginations.

    b. Teens will have trouble going beyond narrative realism in their writing.

    c. Sharing your favorite writers with a teen or young person is a good way to get them to reduce their use of technology.

UNDERSTANDING A STUDY

When you read about a study, think about who did the research, what their purpose was, and how the study was done. This can help you evaluate the study and its results.

Use information from pages 58–60 to note key points of the research.

Study published in (journal): _____

Study carried out by (institutions): _____

Purpose of study: _____

_____

Method

• What was analyzed? _____

• Time periods studied: _____

Findings

• rise in _____

• decline in _____

Interpretation (possible reasons)—Kim, 2011: _____

_____

CRITICAL THINKING

Interpreting. How might the reasons given by Kim account for the findings? Can you think of any other interpretations?

ANALYZING LITERARY EXCERPTS

Excerpts from literary fiction can help give a sense of a story's themes and characters. You may also be able to infer aspects of the plot, and make predictions about what happens next.

A. **Read again the excerpt from *The Veldt* and answer the questions.**

   1. What can we infer about the "nursery"?

      a. It's a large building in an African jungle.

      b. It's a device for traveling back in time.

      c. It's a room that can change its appearance.

   2. What clues in the excerpt led you to your answer? Share your ideas with a partner.

B. **Read again the excerpt from *The Specialist's Hat* and note answers to the questions. Then share your ideas with a partner.**

   1. What can we infer about Claire and Samantha?

      they are twins, Clair is better at being dead than Samantha

   2. What do you think is happening in this excerpt? *pedazo de parrafo.*

      they are talking about dead with their babysitter

   3. What do you think might happen later in the story?

      Sombody will die.

BUILDING VOCABULARY

A. **Use these words from the passage on pages 58–61 to complete the definitions.**

dimensions	distinct	highlight	identical	proficiency

distancia   xearce   Identico   competencia.

   1. If a thing is _distinct_, it is separate or different from other things.

   2. Two people or things that are _identical_ are exactly alike.

   3. A person who has _proficiency_ in a certain area does it with skill and expertise.

   4. If you _highlight_ something, you emphasize it.

   5. If you see something in three _dimensions_ it looks solid because it has length, breadth, and depth.

B. **Complete the paragraph with the words below.**

analyzing   genre   obviously   options   societal

Dystopian worlds—imaginary societies characterized by human misery and conflict—

have been a popular trend in young adult literature for the past couple of decades. For

example, in Suzanne Collins's *The Hunger Games*, much of the population lives in

extreme poverty, and teens face a harsh reality with limited _options_ regarding their

1

future. So why has this kind of dystopian literature become so popular?

Experts _analyzing_ young adult literature say that teens these days are more sensitive

2

to issues such as social injustice and climate change. _Obviously_ people have faced

3

societal and environmental issues for decades, but the growth in popularity of the

4

dystopian _genre_ may reflect the increased insecurity that many young people feel

5

about the future.

A gloomy view of London, England. Dystopian stories are often set in a dark, alternate reality where the normal rules of society have broken down.

C. **Discuss the following questions with a partner.**

1. What are some of your **options** for the future; for example, regarding your career, places to live, places to travel, and so on?

2. In what skill do you have the most **proficiency**? How did you acquire this proficiency?

GETTING MEANING FROM CONTEXT

A. **Find the phrases in bold in the passage on pages 58–60. Study their contexts. Then choose the meanings below that are the closest to the meanings in the passage.**

1. **hallmarks (of something)** (Paragraph 3)

   a. unusual features

   b. typical features

   c. recent features

2. **pulls you out of** (Paragraph 6)

   a. increases your interest in

   b. draws you upwards

   c. takes you away from

3. **plant seeds (of something)** (Paragraph 6)

   a. give an idea about something

   b. cause something to end

   c. complicate something

B. **What are some other ways to plant seeds of inspiration in young people's minds?**

Talk about it and give examples just share

information

CRITICAL THINKING

Personalizing. Discuss these questions with a partner.

1. Which of the books that Laura McClure recommends on page 61 would you like to read? Why?

2. What other books would you recommend for teenagers?

EXPLORE MORE

Read more of Laura McClure's recommendations at blog.ted.com. Share what you learn with the class.

TEDTALKS

THE MYSTERY BOX

J.J. ABRAMS Filmmaker, TED speaker

Known for the emotion he brings to larger-than-life stories, filmmaker J.J. Abrams's work includes a sense of mystery and wonder.

Raised in Los Angeles by entertainment-industry parents, J.J. Abrams began his career in filmmaking during college, when he wrote his first screenplay for the comedy *Taking Care of Business* (1990). He went on to direct several blockbusters, including *Mission: Impossible III*, *Star Trek,* and *Star Wars Episode VII: The Force Awakens*. Abrams writes, directs, and produces in both the television and film industries, and his work covers a range of genres, from action and drama to science fiction.

As a child, Abrams was fascinated with magic. In his TED Talk, he describes how a childhood trip to a magic store with his grandfather sparked his love of mystery. In an interview with *The Telegraph*, Abrams said, "Magic is something that's informed what I've done. The magic that works, to me, is the magic that feels completely grounded and real and tangible, and movies and television are extensions of that."

---

screenplay: *n.* the script for a movie

blockbuster: *n.* a movie that is a big success

grounded: *adj.* realistic

tangible: *adj.* touchable; real

In this lesson, you are going to watch segments of Abrams's TED Talk. Use the information above about Abrams to answer each question.

1. What types of movies and TV shows does Abrams create?

Fittior, mystery ANd Acion

Abrams's **idea worth spreading** is that good storytelling must include mystery (perhaps more important than knowledge) because it represents infinite possibility and hope.

2. What childhood experience inspired Abrams's love of mystery?

Things That his grandfather us doing
like see How thing Works for Ex. The radio

3. How does Abrams describe the type of magic that he likes to use in his work?

Imagination Things, Creative and
Simple Things

PART 1

THE MAGIC BOX

PREDICTING

In his TED Talk, J.J. Abrams starts by talking about a "magic box" that he got as a child (see the photo on page 67). What do you think is inside the box? Where might he have gotten it? Check your answers as you watch (▶) the first segment of his talk.

UNDERSTANDING KEY DETAILS

Read the excerpt. Then complete the sentences that express the key ideas of this part of the talk.

❝ And I realized that I haven't opened [the magic box] because it represents something important—to me. It represents my grandfather. [. . .] But the thing is, that it [also] represents infinite possibility. It represents hope. It represents potential. And what I love about this box [. . .] is I find myself drawn to infinite possibility, that sense of potential. And I realize that mystery is the catalyst for imagination. Now, it's not the most ground-breaking idea, but when I started to think that maybe there are times when mystery is more important than knowledge, I started getting interested in this. ❯❯

---

catalyst: *n.* a person, an idea, an event, or a thing that sparks important changes

groundbreaking: *adj.* innovative

1. To Abrams, the magic box represents _____.

   a. his work as a director   **b.** things that might happen

2. The idea of infinite possibility _____.

   a. inspires Abrams's work   **b.** came from Abrams's movies

3. To Abrams, mystery is _____.

   a. the key aspect of knowledge   **b.** a key aspect of imagination

CRITICAL THINKING

Inferring. Why do you think Abrams has never opened the magic box? Discuss with a partner.

PART 2

CREATION IS EVERYWHERE

PREVIEWING

A. **Discuss with a partner your answers to these questions.**

1. What are some recent examples of visual effects (or special effects) in movies?

2. In your opinion, can anyone make a movie? Why, or why not?

B. **Watch (▶) this segment of the TED Talk and think about your answers above.**

UNDERSTANDING KEY DETAILS

A. **Read the excerpts below from Abrams's talk. Then answer the questions.**

1. **❝** This is an online [video] done by guys who had some visual effects experience. But the point was, that they were doing things that were using these mystery boxes that they had—everyone has now. [. . .] He's doing stuff that looks as amazing as stuff I've seen released from Hollywood. **❯❯**

   What is the "mystery box" that "everyone has now"?

   a. A video camera   **b.** Computer software   **c.** A film stage

2. **❝** The most incredible sort of mystery, I think, is now the question of what comes next. Because it is now democratized. So now, the creation of media is everywhere. **❯❯**

   When Abrams says that the creation of media is now "democratized," what does he mean?

   a. People can elect to see any movie they want, not just Hollywood movies.

   b. Making good special effects is no longer something limited to Hollywood.

   c. Hollywood is letting everyone use the special effects technology they created.

B. **Read the excerpts below and discuss answers to the questions with a partner.**

1. **❝** When I think of the filmmakers who exist out there now who would have been silenced, you know—who have been silenced in the past—it's a very exciting thing. **❯❯**

   Why does Abrams say some filmmakers were "silenced in the past"?

2. **❝** [N]ow I can say, 'Go make your movie!' There's nothing stopping you from going out there and getting the technology. You can lease, rent, buy stuff off the shelf that is either as good, or just as good, as the stuff that's being used by the . . . 'legit people.' **❯❯**

   ---

   legit: *adj.* legitimate: real, accepted, or official

   Why does Abrams believe anyone can now make a movie?

PART 3

CREATIVE PROBLEM-SOLVING

PREVIEWING

Read the following excerpt from this part of the talk and look at the movie poster on page 71. What do you know—or what can you infer—about the movie?

❝ When I did *Mission: Impossible III*, we had amazing visual effects stuff. ILM did the effects; it was incredible. And sort of like my dream to be involved. And there are a couple of sequences in the movie, like these couple of moments I'll show you. ❞

ILM: *n.* Industrial Light and Magic, a visual effects company founded by George Lucas, the creator of *Star Wars* film series

sequences: *n.* parts or scenes in a movie or TV show

ANALYZING PROBLEMS AND SOLUTIONS

A. **Watch (▶) this segment of the TED Talk. What problem did Abrams need to solve? How did he solve it? Write your answers below.**

Problem: *Put A Gun in Tom' Noise was Hurting him*

Solution: *Make Tom put the gun on his noise so that way he know how much pression put into without hurt*

B. **Abrams says: "So you don't need the greatest technology to do things that can work in movies." How does Abrams's solution support this idea? Discuss your answer with a partner.**

CRITICAL THINKING

Synthesizing. Would Abrams agree with the Harvard researchers that the "app generation" has lost its creativity? Why, or why not? What might Abrams say about the potential this generation has?

EXPLORE MORE

Find out more about Abrams's mystery box by watching his full TED Talk at TED.com. Share what you learn with the class.

TOM CRUISE
M:I:III
THE MISSION BEGINS MAY 5

A. **Work with a partner. Think about a story that you could tell using only the technology that you have at hand; for example, your phone or your computer.**

1. Plan a general outline for your story. Who is it about? What happens first, what happens after that, and how does it end?

2. Decide on the best media for your story. Will it be in pictures (like a cartoon or a graphic novel)? Will it be a sound recording? Will it be a movie or a TV show?

3. Then choose your "magic box": your computer, your phone, or your tablet.

4. What applications does your magic box already have that you can use to tell your story; for example, a (video) camera, a voice recorder, a drawing program?

5. Research some additional applications that you could use to tell your story such as drawing and painting apps; music, film, and photo editing software; and so on.

B. **Create a two-minute presentation on your story, the media you have chosen, and how you would use technology to tell it. If possible, use the media to create a short scene from your story that you can include in your presentation.**

C. **Work with two other pairs.**

- Give your presentations.
- As you listen, take notes.
- At the end, review your notes.
- Take a class vote. Which story idea do you like the best? Which idea is best suited to the media and the technology that the presenters chose? Why?

EXPLORE MORE

Learn more about storytelling at TED.com. Watch the TED Talks on the "How to tell a story" playlist. Share what you learn with the class.

HOPE AND EQUALITY

Children take a break at the Krousar Thmey Center for Deprived Children in Phnom Penh, Cambodia. The center brings hope to some of the poorest children in the area by providing them with a safe place to sleep, play, and attend school.

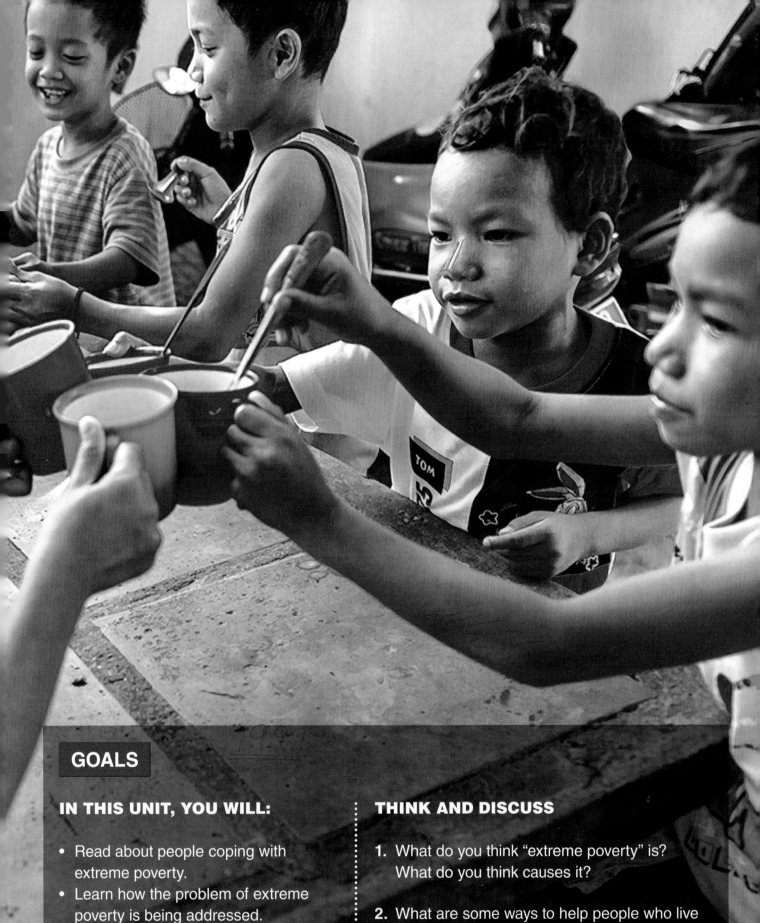

GOALS

IN THIS UNIT, YOU WILL:

- Read about people coping with extreme poverty.
- Learn how the problem of extreme poverty is being addressed.
- Explore statistics about a topic related to poverty.

THINK AND DISCUSS

1. What do you think "extreme poverty" is? What do you think causes it?

2. What are some ways to help people who live in poverty?

PRE-READING

A. **Look at the map and answer the questions with a partner.**

1. Which parts of the world have the lowest income?

    Africa,

2. How much do the poorest people in these areas earn? Do you think you could live on this amount?

    $995 or less a year

B. **Look at the photos and read the captions on pages 77 and 78. What do you think these people's daily lives are like? What might be some of the challenges they face? Discuss your ideas with a partner.**

C. **The passage is an interview with Renée C. Byer. Read the introduction on page 75. Then answer the questions.**

1. Who is Renée C. Byer?

    A photographer

2. What does she do? What effects does she hope her work will have?

    Capture the circumstances of
    people living in extreme poverty.
    Show the way of the live
    of other people

Cope : survive
tolerate

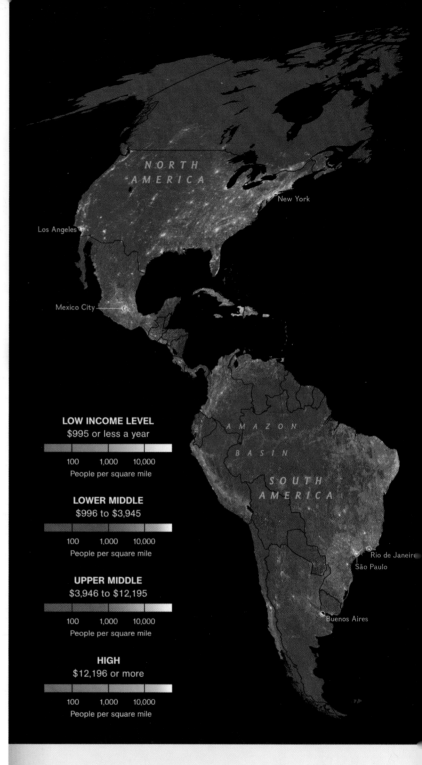

LOW INCOME LEVEL
$995 or less a year

| | | |
| 100 | 1,000 | 10,000 |
People per square mile

LOWER MIDDLE
$996 to $3,945

| | | |
| 100 | 1,000 | 10,000 |
People per square mile

UPPER MIDDLE
$3,946 to $12,195

| | | |
| 100 | 1,000 | 10,000 |
People per square mile

HIGH
$12,196 or more

| | | |
| 100 | 1,000 | 10,000 |
People per square mile

LIVING ON A DOLLAR A DAY

BECKY HARLAN, National Geographic

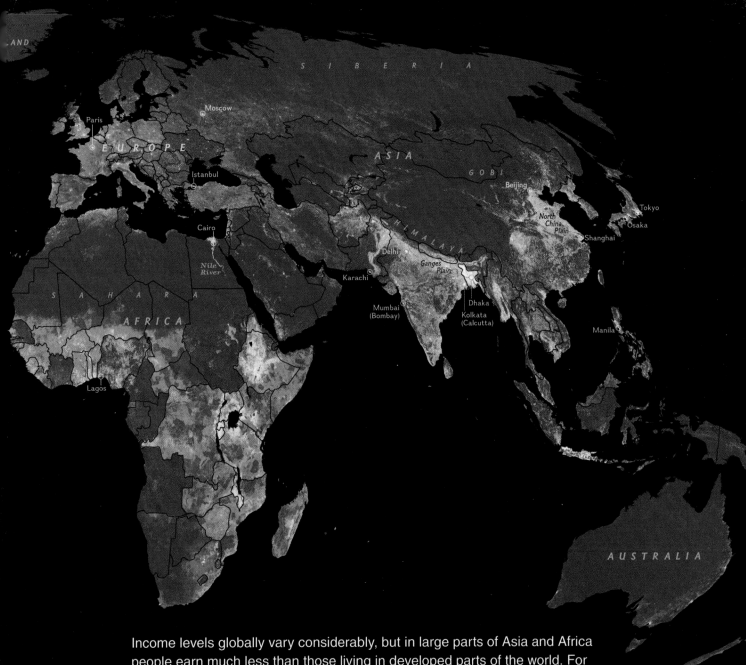

Income levels globally vary considerably, but in large parts of Asia and Africa people earn much less than those living in developed parts of the world. For example, people in some parts of central Africa earn less than $995 a year—or less than $3 a day; in the poorest regions, people earn less than a dollar a day.

1 Approximately one out of six people worldwide live on a dollar a day. It's a statistic that remains abstract for many who do not feel its **implications** on a day-to-day basis. That's why photographer Renée C. Byer traveled to four continents to capture the **circumstances** of people living in extreme poverty—to give us the names and show us the faces of those it haunts. She shows us the poor whose lives are dominated by health problems that are treatable with modern medicine, who work hard in hazardous conditions for little pay, and who build homes on borrowed land because, like all human beings, they have to live somewhere. In her book *Living on a Dollar a Day*, Byer translates a stark statistic into stories that help us more easily connect with the problem of poverty and feel **compassion** for the people it affects. Byer is interviewed by Becky Harlan.

BECKY: *Renée, let's start with Jestina Koko. What is her story?*

2 **RENÉE:** She can't walk, and so she drags herself about her home. Well, she's actually squatting in someone else's home. They're allowing her to sleep in this hallway with her child. I remember that her only hopes and dreams were first, to get herself a place, a little apartment or room that she and her daughter could live in so she wasn't in this trafficky area in this other place, and also that her little girl could go to school. This is a great example of where a child is not able to go to school because she's needed to help her mother. Her mother doesn't have enough money to put her in school. The cycle for her is very grim. Everything is about getting from today to tomorrow. If it wasn't for the **goodwill** of a neighbor, she would be sleeping outside.

allanamiento

traficante

severo

luchar

3 Jestina has **struggled** with this disability since the age of three. So she's living and begging on the sides of the street. When it's raining she can't drag herself out, so she has to work really hard on days when the weather is nice to make up for that. She does laundry for other families, she makes cookies to try and sell, you can see how hard working she is. You see this in almost every country. Nobody is lacking the will to work, they just need a little bit of extra help to get out of the poverty cycle.

Añadir la falta la voluntad de trabajar

BECKY: *You're known for capturing really* **intimate**, *relational moments in your photo essays. Tell me about that.*

4 **RENÉE:** Whether the story is done in the U.S. or abroad, the most important thing is to let it unfold on its own. Time and **access** are the essence of compelling photojournalism. I have this innate curiosity that drives me beyond the obvious. For me, it's very important to go behind the scenes and into their home to find pieces of daily life that everyone can relate to. So people aren't seeing a photo that will push them away, but will pull them back into the scene. So they're not being **overwhelmed** by the emotion, but they're able to relate to the emotion. So that they can imagine themselves trying to live this life, and in some way, hopefully, they could help.

extranjero

desplegar

innato

> **" I think of myself as a journalist who chooses the art of photography to bring awareness to the world. Art . . . combined with journalism has the ability to bring awareness to issues that can elevate understanding and compassion. It's the basic reality of why I do what I do. "**
>
> **—Renée C. Byer**

5 For instance, we were at a slum in Delhi, and I see this little boy scavenging in this horrible garbage wasteland. He's got bare hands, no protective clothing. He's wearing flip-flops, I think. And he's looking for a few rags to sell as material to earn some money for his family. I'm standing there in insufferable heat, my shoes are literally melting it's so hot, and all I'm thinking about, focusing on, is how can I tell this story about this little boy? No one else can smell this terrible smell that I'm smelling, nobody can feel this intense heat, nobody can imagine this wasteland that I'm standing in. How can I give this justice in a photograph? That's what's going on in my head. I'm trying very hard in my head to translate that to someone who has never been there.

6 Later on, I went inside his family's home. I had no idea what the inside of any of these places was like, so I was just stunned that it was this one tiny 10' x 10' room with just a bed. That was their entire living space. And these boys just started playing on the bed. It was such a beautiful slice of life. It's one of those moments that's so **unexpected** that you just feel privileged to be witness of. To me, it was such an interesting dichotomy between this child and his determination to try to find something

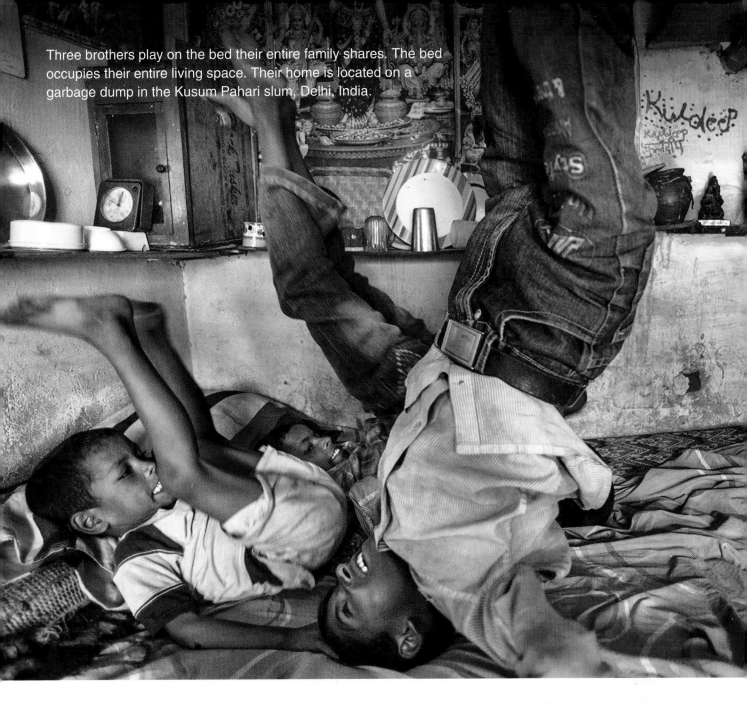

Three brothers play on the bed their entire family shares. The bed occupies their entire living space. Their home is located on a garbage dump in the Kusum Pahari slum, Delhi, India.

to help his family survive and then later in the day having him play in this very childlike way on the bed with his brothers, and it was this range of emotion which is so important in this kind of work. It shows how the human spirit can transcend even the worst deprivation.

BECKY: *Renée, what effect do you hope your work will have?*

7 **RENÉE:** It's very, very easy to look at these images as if they're not real, but they are real. This does exist. The biggest challenge is making that connection, so that people understand that there are 18,000 children

under the age of five dying every day from causes that are preventable. I'm serious. How can that be happening in this day and age? And that's why this book is a call to action. I hope in my lifetime that we can make a difference, and **eradicate** this—that we can have a shared humanity.

---

hazardous: *adj.* dangerous

squatting: *v.* occupying an unused building or piece of land

scavenging: *v.* searching for food or objects that other people may have thrown away

transcend: *v.* to go beyond or above a measure or standard

deprivation: *n.* a condition of want and need

dichotomy: *n.* a great difference between two things

Jestina Koko and her daughter, Satta Quaye, live in Monrovia, Liberia. Physically disabled since the age of three, Jestina depends on her arms to lift and drag herself. She survives by doing laundry for others, selling cookies on the street, and begging.

GETTING THE MAIN IDEAS

Check (✔) the three sentences that best summarize the main ideas expressed in the interview on pages 76–77.

_____ **1.** Byer believes that Jestina and her child will be able to break the cycle of poverty because of a neighbor's kindness.

✔ **2.** Byer believes that showing the private moments in life is the best way to help people feel connected with her subjects.

✔ **3.** Byer hopes her book will inspire people to get involved with activities that will help end extreme poverty.

_____ **4.** Byer felt that the best way to portray the life of the boy in Delhi was to show him working in the garbage dump.

✔ **5.** Byer believes that photography combined with journalism is an effective way to help people notice and feel compassion for people who live in poverty.

UNDERSTANDING KEY DETAILS

A. Complete the chart with details about the people described in the passage.

Person	What kind of place does the person live in?	What does the person do to survive?	What other hardships does the person have to deal with?
(Liberia) Jestina	. her neighboard's house	. she does loundry . She sell cookies on the streets.	. Disable, . She can't walk
(India) The little boy	In a 10 x 10 room	. he scavange in garbage waste land.	has no protective clothing

B. What aspects of the people's lives most affected Byer? Discuss with a partner.

PARAPHRASING INFORMATION

Find the following sentences in the passage. Read the sentences around them.
Then choose the best paraphrase for each sentence.

1. "Nobody is lacking the will to work, they just need a little bit of extra help to get out of the poverty cycle." (Paragraph 3)

    a. With some help, people can get out of the poverty cycle to do the work they want to do.

    b. The cycle of poverty keeps people poor, and they cannot get out of it no matter how much help they get.

2. "For me, it's very important to go behind the scenes and into their home to find pieces of daily life that everyone can relate to." (Paragraph 4)

    a. Byer feels that people will be more interested in helping the poor if she avoids realistic scenes showing how they actually live.

    b. Byer believes that it's a good idea to take pictures of everyday life among the poor because it helps other people to better relate to them.

    → two parts of something

3. "To me, it was such an interesting dichotomy between this child and his determination to try to find something to help his family survive and then later in the day having him play in this very childlike way on the bed with his brothers . . ." (Paragraph 6)

    a. Byer was fascinated by the contrast between the boy's adult like sense of responsibility to his family and how much he still enjoyed playing like a child.

    b. Byer noticed that the boy's struggle to help his family survive did not give him an opportunity to enjoy his childhood.

BUILDING VOCABULARY

A. **Complete the paragraph with these words from the passage. One word is extra.**

remove → *erradicar*

access   *cutout* → **eradicate** (V)   **implications** (N)   **unexpected**

One way to help __eradicate__ poverty is to improve __access__ to electricity in
1 2

developing nations. However, as poor countries develop, their contributions to global

greenhouse gas emissions can rise. One way to address this problem is a development

strategy called Green Growth, where environmentally friendly practices are put in place

as countries improve their standards of living. In Nicaragua, for example, there's a project

bulbs

to install compact-fluorescent (CFL) light bulbs in homes, schools, and other buildings in

two small villages. Because of these kinds of projects, household energy use actually

dropped nearly 30 percent. Daniel Kammen, chief technical specialist at the World Bank,

summarizes the project's __implications__: "It shows that you can meet development
3

objectives for the poor and climate objectives for all of us at the same time."

B. **Find the words in bold below in the passage on pages 75–77. Read the
words around them to guess their meanings. Then match the words to
the correct definitions.**

1. _c_ **struggle**   a. warm and private
2. _e_ **circumstances**   b. affected very strongly
3. _a_ **intimate**   c. to use a lot of physical or mental effort and energy to do something
4. _d_ **goodwill**   d. helpful, cooperative feelings
5. _b_ **overwhelmed**   e. conditions of someone's life

C. **Choose the best prepositions to complete each sentence.**

1. Byer hopes her images inspire people to **feel compassion** by / (for) people who live in
   extreme poverty.

2. Even in wealthy nations, people still **struggle** for / (with) poverty, especially in
   countries that do not provide adequate welfare for their citizens.

3. When you **feel overwhelmed** (by) / toward all the problems in the world, the best thing
   to do is to take action.

4. Byer's images help create feelings of **goodwill** (for) / with people who are
   less fortunate.

GETTING MEANING FROM CONTEXT

A. **Find the following sentences in context in the passage on pages 75–77. Choose the best definitions for the phrases in bold.**

1. "It's a statistic that remains abstract for many who do not feel its implications **on a day-to-day basis**." (paragraph 1)

   a. all day long   **b.** every day   **c.** for one day only

2. "It was such a beautiful **slice of life**." (paragraph 6)

   a. positive attitude   **b.** realistic, everyday view   **c.** unusual situation

B. **Write answers to the following questions. Then discuss your answers with a partner.**

1. Are there any daily challenges in your life? What affects you on a **day-to-day basis**? How does it affect you?

   _____

   _____

2. Can you think of a TV show or movie that shows a **slice of life** for the poor? Describe it.

   _Slumdog Millionaire_____

   _____

CRITICAL THINKING

Interpreting. Discuss the following questions with a partner.

1. What does Renée Byer mean when she says, "And that's why this book is a call to action. I hope in my lifetime that we can make a difference, and eradicate this—that we can have a shared humanity"?

2. Do you think that Byer's images can actually motivate people to action? Why or why not?

EXPLORE MORE

Search for more of Byer's photos online. Which images do you think are particularly powerful? Share your ideas with the class.

TEDTALKS

THE GOOD NEWS ON POVERTY (YES, THERE'S GOOD NEWS)

BONO Activist, TED speaker

🎧 "Exit the rock star. Enter . . . the factivist," declares Bono at the start of his TED Talk. The Irish-born lead singer of U2 is on a worldwide mission to end hunger, extreme poverty, and disease.

From his early days as a rock performer, Bono has used his celebrity status to raise awareness of important issues. While news associated with extreme poverty has typically been bad, Bono has good news. He believes that we are making significant progress in addressing this problem. For example, since 2000, there are 8 million more AIDS patients getting life-saving antiretroviral drugs, eight countries in sub-Saharan Africa have cut death rates from malaria by 75 percent, and childhood mortality rates are down by 2.65 million a year. He has seen some of this firsthand through his work with organizations such as the ONE Campaign, which fights extreme poverty, especially in Africa.

---

activist: *n.* a person who works at changing something, especially in politics

factivist: *n.* a term Bono created to mean an activist who uses facts

antiretroviral drugs: *n.* drugs that fight the AIDS virus

childhood mortality: *n.* the death of children under the age of five

Bono's **idea worth spreading** is that we can eradicate poverty by 2030 if we really believe in our own collective momentum.

In this lesson, you are going to watch segments of Bono's TED Talk.
Use the information about Bono on page 82 to answer each question.

1. Why might Bono be in a position to influence people?

   _____

2. What three facts support Bono's statement that we are reducing extreme poverty?

   _____

   _____

   _____

TEDTALKS

THE GOOD NEWS . . .

PREVIEWING

Read this excerpt from Bono's talk. Then choose the best answer to the question that follows.

> ❰❰ For kids under five, child mortality [is] down by 2.65 million a year. That's a rate of 7,256 children's lives saved each day. Wow. . . . Let's just stop for a second, actually, and think about that. Have you read anything anywhere in the last week that is remotely as important as that number? Wow. Great news. It drives me nuts that most people don't seem to know this news. ❱❱

---

drives (someone) nuts: *idiom* bothers and annoys them

What is annoying Bono?

a. There is too much bad news about poverty and very little progress.

b. There is very little news about poverty, and this is making the problem worse.

c. There is good news about poverty, but few people are aware of it.

UNDERSTANDING MAIN IDEAS

Watch (▶) the first segment of Bono's TED Talk. Choose the correct word or phrase to complete the summary of his main ideas.

The facts show that progress has been made in **reducing / documenting** extreme poverty. In fact, the percentage of people living in extreme poverty **fell by 30% / halved** between 1990 and 2010. While the number is still **high / uncertain,** if the trend continues, we should be able to eradicate poverty completely.

UNDERSTANDING GRAPHS

Study the graph that Bono uses in this part of the talk on page 85, and read the caption. Then answer the questions.

1. What does the graph show?

   _____

2. What do you think *trajectory* means in this context?

   _____

3. What does Zero Zone 2028 mean?

   The poverty can be eradicated by 2028

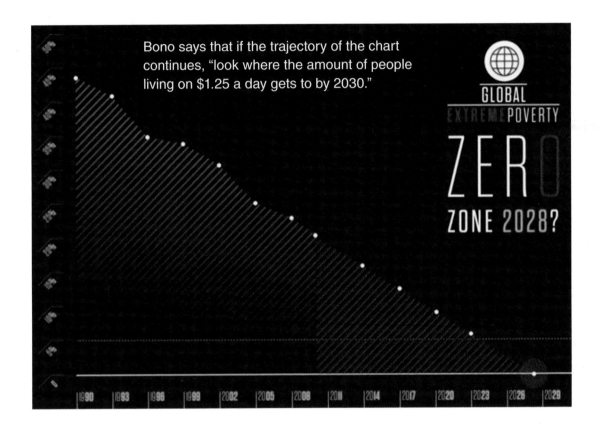

Bono says that if the trajectory of the chart continues, "look where the amount of people living on $1.25 a day gets to by 2030."

GLOBAL EXTREME POVERTY

ZERO

ZONE 2028?

CRITICAL THINKING

Analyzing. Look again at the graph above. What are the steps that you think could be taken to get to the zero zone?

PART 2

FIGHTING CORRUPTION

UNDERSTANDING PROBLEMS AND SOLUTIONS

A. **Read the following excerpt from this part of the talk, and answer the questions.**

> « Right now today, in Oslo as it happens, oil companies are fighting to keep secret their payments to governments for extracting oil in developing countries. [. . .] And right now, we know that the biggest disease of all is not a disease. It's corruption. But there's a vaccine for that, too. It's called transparency, open data sets. [. . .] Daylight, you could call it, transparency. »

---

corruption: *n.* dishonest activities   **transparency:** *n.* openness, especially in government

1. According to Bono, what is the biggest "disease" we are fighting right now?

    a. Poverty   **b.** Corruption   **c.** Transparency

2. How does he think oil companies contribute to this disease? Underline the answer in the excerpt.

B. Watch (▶) the next segment of Bono's talk. What problems does Bono describe in this part of the talk? What solutions does he propose? Complete the chart below.

a. need transparency in budgets and spending

d. reduce the Global Fund

b. join the ONE Campaign to push for new laws

e. tell politicians that these cuts cost lives

c. oil companies' secret payments

f. government corruption

PROBLEMS		SOLUTIONS
	→	
	→	
	→	

SUMMARIZING MAIN IDEAS

Choose the best paraphrase of the main ideas in this part of the talk.

_____ **a.** Most people aren't motivated enough to help solve the problems that cause extreme poverty. However, there are new technologies that will help us attain the goal of getting extreme poverty down to zero in the future.

_____ **b.** There are several problems that could prevent us from meeting the goal of zero percent level of extreme poverty. However, if we act collectively to solve these problems, that goal is attainable.

CRITICAL THINKING

Analyzing / Evaluating. Discuss the following questions with a partner.

1. What do you think are the root causes of extreme poverty?

_____

_____

2. Which method do you think works better in raising awareness about poverty—Bono's factivism or Byer's photos? Explain.

_____

_____

EXPLORE MORE

Find out more about Bono's news on eradicating poverty. Watch his full talk at TED.com. Share what you learn with the class.

Children at a primary school in rural Cambodia use a hand pump donated by a local charitable association. The pump provides drinking water as well as access to sanitation.

Project

A. You are going to present an infographic about a topic related to poverty. Work with a partner to follow the steps below.

1. Choose one of the following topics to research.

   - differences in income levels
   - child mortality rates
   - access to education (e.g., primary school enrollment or secondary school graduation)
   - literacy rates
   - access to clean water

2. Research statistics about your chosen topic. Find out how the rates or levels have changed over a period of time.

3. Create an infographic that illustrates your findings. For example, you could create a line graph similar to the one Bono used in his talk.

B. Work with two other pairs and follow the steps below.

   - Present your infographic to your group.
   - As you listen to other presentations, take notes.
   - Ask and answer questions about each infographic.

C. As a class, discuss the following questions.

1. Which infographic has the most surprising information? Why is it surprising?
2. Does the infographic change your thinking or attitudes in any way? Explain.

EXPLORE MORE

Learn more about the ONE campaign Bono mentioned in his TED Talk. Go to ONE.org and read about other issues the organization is concerned with. Share what you learn with the class.

BACKING UP HISTORY

GOALS

IN THIS UNIT, YOU WILL:

- Read about natural and man-made forces endangering historic sites.
- Learn about a person who uses technology to preserve these sites.
- Explore historic sites worth saving.

THINK AND DISCUSS

1. Look at the photo and read the caption. What is happening?

2. Why do you think we should preserve historical sites?

At Mission Dolores—the oldest surviving building in San Francisco, U.S.A.—a laser fires 50,000 beams a second up and down a wall, making a 3-D model of an earthquake-threatened structure.

PRE-READING

A. **Read the caption and first paragraph on this page. Then answer these questions with a partner.**

1. What do you see in the photos?

   _____

2. What do you think the passage is about?

   _____

B. **Scan the information on page 92 and then answer the questions below.**

1. In which country can you find each place?

   Rosslyn Chapel ___Scotland___

   The Eastern Qing Tombs ___China___

   Mount Rushmore ___USA - South Dacota___

2. What is or was the primary purpose of each place? Use the words below.[1]

   a. burial ground

   b. monument

   c. place of worship

   ___C___ Rosslyn Chapel

   ___a___ The Eastern Qing Tombs

   ___b___ Mount Rushmore

3. Why do you think these places are included in this reading passage? Discuss with a partner.

The Royal Kasubi Tombs in the kingdom of Buganda, Uganda, were destroyed by fire. Fortunately, a company named CyArk had made detailed scans of the building. Within days of the fire, a Buganda prince was talking to CyArk about rebuilding the historic site.

1 In 2014, a fire completely destroyed Uganda's Royal Kasubi Tombs. The 700-year-old wood-and-thatch tombs were the ritual burial place of four kings and were an important part of Ugandan history. It seemed as though this **sacred** place—a UNESCO world heritage **site**—might be gone forever. But all was not lost.

LASER PRESERVATION

2 Two years before the fire, CyArk, an organization that collects detailed digital records of cultural **heritage** sites, had created a "copy" of the site. By digitally **preserving** the tombs, there was enough information to rebuild and **thereby** preserve this historically important site for future generations.

3 Over 800 World Heritage sites like the Royal Kasubi Tombs are currently at risk. Many are **deteriorating** at a rapid rate. Age, weather, and general wear and tear are factors. Natural disasters such as earthquakes—and frequently **occurring** man-made destruction—also take their toll. But digital scanning technology—like that used by CyArk—is coming to the rescue.

4 CyArk founder and TED speaker Ben Kacyra was one of the inventors of the scanning technology. He was inspired to start CyArk after the Taliban demolished Afghanistan's Bamiyan Buddhas in 2001 (see page 103). If detailed scans are available, he reasoned, at least there will be some sort of record if disaster strikes.

5 CyArk has a goal of recording 500 world heritage sites, and has already completed scans of 40 of them. These sites include Rosslyn Chapel, the Eastern Qing Tombs, and Mount Rushmore.

---

thatch: *adj. reeds, straw, or leaves used to make a roof*

take their toll: *idiom to cause harm*

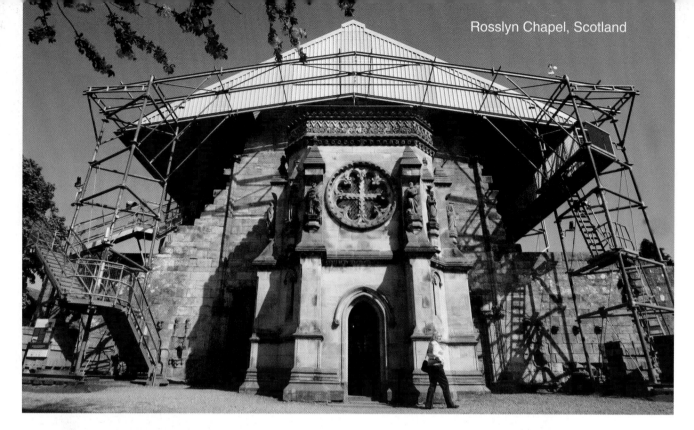

ROSSLYN CHAPEL

6 Rosslyn Chapel, located in Scotland, is one of CyArk's completed projects. Built of stone in the 15th century, this place of worship is famous for its intricate **symbolic** carvings. It has faced many threats over its 600-year history. It was partially destroyed in 1551, used as a stable in 1650, and more recently, an intruder damaged one of the chapel's pillars with a pickax. Now that the stones have been scanned, future damage can be repaired.

THE EASTERN QING TOMBS

7 The Eastern Qing Tombs are an elaborate royal burial ground in China. Built in the 17th century, it houses the resting places of five Qing Dynasty emperors and 15 empresses. CyArk has scanned the elaborate carvings and statues that decorate the tombs as part of a program they call the Scottish Ten, a project that aims to produce virtual reproductions of ten world-class cultural sites. CyArk's scans of the Qing tombs offer a glimpse into the funeral practices of the era.

MOUNT RUSHMORE

8 Mt. Rushmore, in South Dakota, U.S.A., is one of CyArk's more challenging projects. Completed in 1941, sculptors took 14 years to carve the heads of presidents George Washington, Thomas Jefferson, Theodore Roosevelt, and Abraham Lincoln into the side of the mountain. In 2010, a CyArk team scanned the giant sculpted heads over 16 days. Besides dealing with fog, rain, snow, and hail, the team had to climb up to the top of the 5,725-foot (1,745 m) rocky mountain in order to take the scans. They then had to rope their equipment into position to scan hard-to-reach places in the monument like chins and eye sockets.

9 CyArk continues to scan and record important historic sites. A network of 38 international partners is helping in the effort. All data collected is archived and publicly available at cyark.org. "Our collective memory is in the works of man," Kacyra says. "This is really not just a matter of preserving this site or that site. It's a matter of preserving our human collective memory."

---

tomb: *n.* a burial room or grave with a monument over it

pickax: *n.* a cutting tool with a sharp metal head on a long wooden handle

POINT CLOUD

MESHING

3-D MODELING

**SCANNER LOCATIONS SHOWN
ON A 3-D DIGITAL MODEL**
- Suspended by ropes
- Tripod mounted
- Tripod mounted; placement
  hidden from view

MAPPING A MONUMENT

10 CyArk's key tool for saving historic sites is a portable 3-D laser scanner. The scanner moves over an area, such as the wall of a tomb, with a pulsing laser. The laser measures points on the surfaces of the area and makes a high-definition record of them, called a "point cloud." The laser records points as close together as every half centimeter. A point cloud can include hundreds of millions of pieces of data about an area. One piece of data is the "intensity return"—the **intensity** of light reflection from the surface. Different colors can show where there are cracks, or whether newer materials have been **incorporated** into the structure. The data points are then joined together in a process called meshing to create a virtual surface. The mesh is then combined with information from digital photographs to create a realistic 3-D model.

GETTING THE MAIN IDEAS

A. **Complete a summary statement that expresses the main idea of the passage as a whole.**

It's important to _preserve_ historic sites for future generations, and a new

technology is helping us do that.

B. **Check (✓) the sentence that best expresses each of the main ideas of the following paragraphs.**

Paragraph 3:

_____ **1.** World heritage sites must be preserved for future generations.

_✓_ **2.** CyArk has developed a technology for preserving at-risk heritage sites.

_____ **3.** CyArk made a digital copy of the Royal Kasubi Tombs before they were destroyed.

Paragraph 4:

_____ **1.** When the Taliban demolished an important heritage site in Afghanistan in 2001, there was no technology to preserve ancient sites.

_✓_ **2.** Kacyra saw the need for a technology that could preserve heritage sites after an important monument was demolished.

_____ **3.** Kacyra wanted a technology that could preserve old places after the Kasubi Tombs were destroyed.

The tomb of Emperor Qianlong is part of the elaborate Eastern Qing Tombs complex in Zunhua, China.

SUMMARIZING KEY DETAILS

Complete the mind map with details about the historic sites described in the passage.

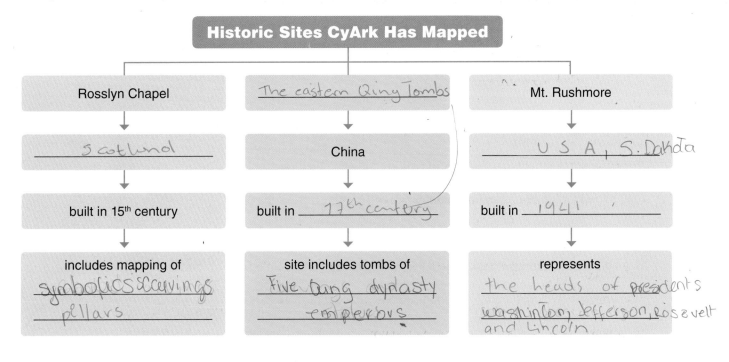

Historic Sites CyArk Has Mapped

Rosslyn Chapel	The eastern Qing Tombs	Mt. Rushmore
Scotland	China	_U S A, S. Dakota_
built in 15th century	built in _17th century_	built in _1941_
includes mapping of _symbolics scarvings pillars_	site includes tombs of _Five Qing dynasty emperors_	represents _the heads of presidents washington, Jefferson, Rosevelt and Lincoln_

UNDERSTANDING A PROCESS

One way to have a better understanding of a technological process is to examine each aspect, and then explain how it works in your own words.

A. Review the information on page 93. Then match the sentence parts.

1. The red and blue dots and the blue circles _e_.

2. The laser scanners measure and record specific _e_.

3. The laser scanners are called "3-D" because they show _h_.

4. A "point cloud" is _g_.

5. The scanner also records information about _b_.

6. Different degrees of intensity can indicate _f_.

7. A computer connects the data points to _c_.

8. By combining a virtual surface with digital photographs, the computer creates _h_.

a. the strength of the light reflection in each point

b. the three dimensions of an object—the length, breadth, and depth

c. create a virtual surface

d. show the location of the scanners

e. points on the surface of the site

f. cracks and different materials in the structure

g. a collection of information about an area on the surface of the site

h. an accurate 3-D model

B. Now complete the summary statement of how CyArk's technology works.

CyArk creates digital _scan models_ of heritage sites by using portable _scanners_ that

scan and record information in three _dimensions_.

BUILDING VOCABULARY

A. **Complete the paragraphs with the words below.**

deteriorate   heritage   preserving   sites   thereby

Nations work hard to get their historic ___sites___ — buildings, wilderness, and
1

ruins—on the World Heritage List. Inclusion on this list can be very valuable to a nation

in terms of generating tourist income. In addition, when an important site is on this list,

there is a commitment to __preserving__ it, __thereby__ ensuring that it will be
2   3

maintained for future generations to enjoy.

How do historic sites get on this list? In November 1972, the United Nations Educational,

Scientific, and Cultural Organization (UNESCO) adopted a treaty known as the World

Heritage Convention. Its goal is to identify cultural and natural places of "outstanding

universal value." In order to qualify, a __heritage__ site must include important historical
4

information that is worth passing on to future generations. If the site—through natural

disaster, war, or lack of funds—begins to __deteriorate__, nations that have signed the
5
↳damage

treaty must assist.
agreement between 2 or more country's.

B. **Read the sentences. Choose the words that are the closest in meaning to the
bold words.**

1. Upon close examination, the researchers noticed that another material—cement—
   had been **incorporated into** the granite sculptures.

   a. included in   **b.** replaced with   **c.** taken out of

2. The color in the scans shows variations in the **intensity** of light reflection in different
   places on the site. For example, green shows one level of reflection, and yellow
   shows another.

   a. warmth   **b.** origin   **c.** strength

3. Kacyra wanted to find a way to preserve historic sites before any more tragic events
   occurred, such as the destruction of the Bamiyan Buddhas.

   a. were discovered   **b.** continued   **c.** happened

4. Experts can only guess at the meaning of some of Rosslyn Chapel's many **symbolic** carvings. For example, they think carvings of small squares with lines and dots may represent musical notes.

   a. representative of something else   **b.** used to show life like images   **c.** used to show creative thinking

5. There are many old **sacred** sites in India that are of immense religious significance to Hindus.

   a. secret   **b.** holy   **c.** unusual

C. **Think of objects you know that have symbolic carvings or other artistic representations incorporated into them; for example, buildings or coins. What are the symbols? What do they represent? Discuss with a partner.**

GETTING MEANING FROM CONTEXT

A. **Find the bold phrases below in the passage. Study their contexts. Then choose the meaning below that is the closest to the meaning in the passage.**

1. **offer a glimpse into** (Paragraph 7)

   a. enable a complete understanding of

   b. raise many questions about

   c. provide a brief experience of

2. **(our) collective memory** (Paragraph 9)

   a. shared memories passed from one generation to the next

   b. the ability of individuals to remember things from the past

   c. the things that our generation has created as a group

B. **What is an example of a collective memory of your family or your culture? Think of stories or traditions that your ancestors have passed on to you. Discuss your answers with a partner.**

CRITICAL THINKING

Reflecting. Discuss the questions with a partner.

1. Who do you think should "own" sites of historical importance in your country?

2. Who should be responsible for looking after them?

3. Who should pay to maintain them?

EXPLORE MORE

Read more about world heritage sites at nationalgeographic.com. Share what you learn with the class.

TEDTALKS

ANCIENT WONDERS CAPTURED IN 3-D

BEN KACYRA Digital preservationist, TED speaker

🔲 Can you imagine a world where few clues to our human history remain? Concerned about how many precious historic sites were under threat, Ben Kacyra founded CyArk. Its mission: to digitally preserve the world's cultural heritage sites.

In the 1990s, Kacyra, an engineer, invented one of the first portable laser scanners designed to measure and map areas of land. Kacyra realized he could use this technology to measure, map, and make 3-D models of at-risk heritage sites. He created CyArk in 2003.

All the data that CyArk collects is archived in an online database at cyark.org, with free access to anyone who wants to use it. Because it is digital, it will last indefinitely, and ongoing improvements in digital scanning technologies will continue to make the information useful for future generations.

---

archived: *adj.* placed in a collection of records and books of historical interest

database: *n.* information on a topic stored in a computer system

In this lesson, you are going to watch segments of Kacyra's TED Talk. Use the information above and what you learned in Lesson A about Kacyra to answer each question.

1. What is CyArk's mission?

    To preserve the history.

2. What technology was CyArk developed from?

    laser scaning

3. How can you see CyArk's scans?

    online / data base.

Ben Kacyra's **idea worth spreading** is that digital technology can help us preserve the world's cultural heritage sites from natural disasters, war, and neglect, safeguarding them for future generations.

GETTING STARTED

PREVIEWING

At the start of his talk, Ben Kacyra tells a story from his childhood. Read the excerpt below. Why do you think he tells this story? Discuss your ideas with a partner.

> ❝ I'd like to start with a short story. It's about a little boy whose father was a history buff and who used to take him by the hand to visit the ruins of an ancient metropolis on the outskirts of their camp. They would always stop by to visit these huge winged bulls that used to guard the gates of that ancient metropolis, and the boy used to be scared of these winged bulls, but at the same time they excited him. And the dad used to use those bulls to tell the boy stories about that civilization and their work. ❞

---

history buff: *n.* a person whose hobby is studying history

outskirts: *n.* the outer area of a town or a city

metropolis: *n.* a large, important city

• Because was there when he starts to like this things.

UNDERSTANDING KEY DETAILS

Check your answers to the Previewing activity as you watch (▶) the first segment of Kacyra's talk. Then complete each statement with the best word or phrase.

1. Traditional surveying equipment is _____ than Kacyra's technology.

   a. heavier   **b.** slower   **c.** more expensive

2. Traditional equipment can capture _____ points in a day.

   a. 50,000   **b.** 5,000   **c.** 500

3. Kacyra's equipment can record _____ points per second.

   a. 10,000   **b.** 1,000   **c.** 1 million

4. Kacyra founded CyArk with _____.

   a. his wife   **b.** a colleague   **c.** his father

5. A _____ partly inspired Kacyra to found CyArk.

   a. Buddhist teacher   **b.** childhood memory   **c.** TV show

CRITICAL THINKING

Interpreting. Kacyra says, ". . . the dad used to use those bulls to tell the boy stories about that civilization and their work." What is Kacyra telling us about the role that places like this can play in our lives?

3-D BENEFITS

IDENTIFYING BENEFITS

Watch (▶) the next segment of Kacyra's TED Talk. Then answer the questions below.

1. Which groups of people benefit most from Kacyra's 3-D models?

_____

_____

2. What are some possible applications of the models?

_____

_____

CRITICAL THINKING

Applying. What other ways do you think Kacyra's technology could be used? Discuss with a partner.

The Hall of Winged Bulls in the Palace of Sargon II, Khorsabad, Iraq. Several monuments like this were destroyed in northern Iraq in 2015.

UNDERSTANDING CAUSES AND EFFECTS

Read the following excerpt and discuss your answers to the questions below with a partner.

> ❝ [I]t became clear to me that we are losing the sites and the stories faster than we can physically preserve them. Of course, earthquakes and all the natural phenomena—floods, tornadoes, etc.—take their toll. However, what occurred to me was human-caused destruction, which was not only causing a significant portion of the destruction, but actually it was accelerating [it]. This includes arson, urban sprawl, acid rain, not to mention terrorism and wars. It was getting more and more apparent that we're fighting a losing battle. We're losing our sites and the stories, and basically we're losing a piece— and a significant piece—of our collective memory. ❞

arson: *n.* the deliberate setting of fires by someone

urban sprawl: *n.* when urban areas expand in an uncontrolled manner

acid rain: *n.* rain that becomes acidic due to industrial emissions. The acid is harmful to the environment and to structures.

1. What does Kacyra say about the pace of destruction? Underline where in the excerpt it tells you.

2. What can cause loss of or damage to historic sites according to Kacyra? Complete the mind map.

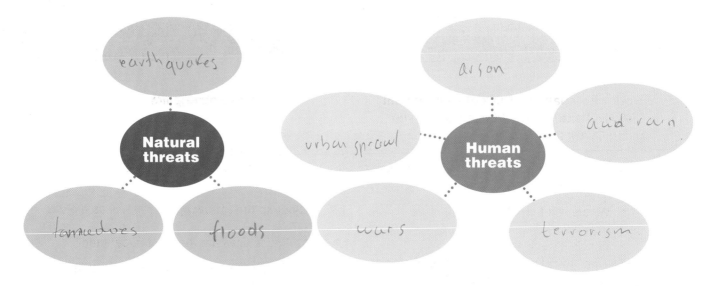

3. According to Kacyra, what do we lose when we lose historic sites?

_____

EXPLORE MORE

Find out more about Kacyra's work at CyArk.org. What is the oldest site the organization is working with? Share what you learn with the class.

Project

1,500-year-old statues of Buddha in Bamiyan, Afghanistan, were deliberately destroyed by the Taliban government in 2001. Many countries have pledged money to rebuild them.

BEFORE 2001

AFTER 2001

A. Work with a partner. Think of an important historical site that ought to be preserved using CyArk technology.

1. With your partner, choose a site. Then answer the following questions.

   - Where is the site?
   - How old is it?
   - Why is it significant?
   - What condition is it in? What human or natural threats are affecting it?
   - How will the site benefit from laser-scanning technology?

2. Create a two-minute presentation on your findings. Include reasons that you think this site should be preserved.

B. Work with two other pairs.

   - Give your presentations.
   - As you listen, take notes.
   - At the end, review your notes.

C. Discuss the following questions as a class.

1. Which sites are the most threatened?

2. Which site is the most deserving of funding for preservation? Why?

EXPLORE MORE

Learn more about how people are using technology to investigate and preserve the past by watching the TED Talks by Rajesh Rao, Sarah Parcak, William Noel, or Eric Sanderson at TED.com. Share what you learn with the class.

Soybeans are harvested at Fartura Farm, in Brazil's Mato Grosso
state. Brazil is the second largest soy producer worldwide.

FOOD
FOR ALL

IN THIS UNIT, YOU WILL:

- Read about ways to feed a growing global population.
- Learn how food production and delivery systems affect cities.
- Explore ways to change your relationship with food.

THINK AND DISCUSS

1. Think about the food that you ate today. Do you know how or where it was produced?

2. What effects might food production have on the environment?

PRE-READING

A. **Look at the photos on the right and on the previous page, and read the captions. Then discuss the questions below with a partner.**

1. What food is being produced in each photo?

2. What do you think are the differences between large-scale and small-scale farming methods?

B. **Read the title and introduction on this page. Then note your answers to the following questions.**

1. Who do you think are the "nine billion"?

_____

2. What are the possible challenges of feeding these nine billion?

_____

_____

3. Why might the author think that "food poses one of the biggest dangers to the planet"?

_____

_____

_____

C. **Read the headings on page 108. What kind of information do you think this section will contain?**

_____

_____

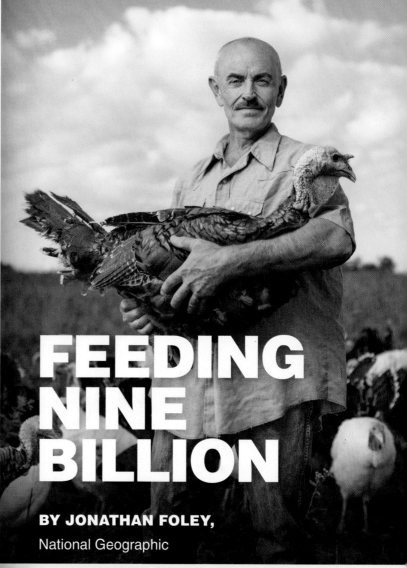

FEEDING NINE BILLION

BY JONATHAN FOLEY,
National Geographic

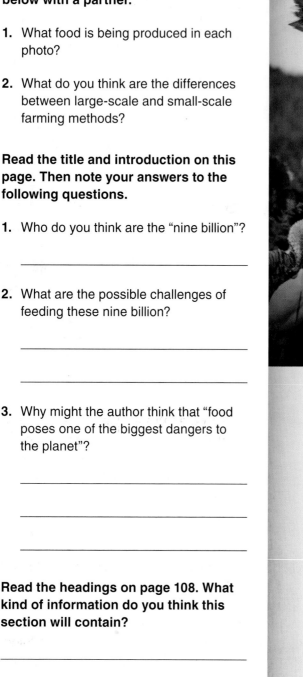

 When we think about threats to the environment, we tend to picture cars and smokestacks—not dinner. But the truth is, our need for food **poses** one of the biggest dangers to the planet.

1 Agriculture is among the greatest contributors to global warming, **emitting** more greenhouse gases than all our cars, trucks, trains, and airplanes combined—largely from methane released by cattle and rice farms, nitrous oxide from fertilized fields, and carbon dioxide from the cutting of rain forests to grow crops or raise livestock. Farming is the thirstiest user of our precious water supplies and a major polluter, as runoff from fertilizers and manure disrupts fragile lakes, rivers, and coastal ecosystems across the globe. Agriculture also **accelerates** the loss of biodiversity: As we've

Small farms play a big role in feeding the world, particularly in the developing world. *(Left)* Frank Reese raises turkeys on his farm in Lindsborg, Kansas, U.S.A. *(Middle)* Mariam Kéita harvests peanuts on a farm in Siby, Mali. *(Right)* High up in the Peruvian mountains, Estela Cóndor grows potatoes to sell at market.

cleared areas of grassland and forest for farms, we've lost crucial habitat, making agriculture a major driver of wildlife extinction.

2 The environmental challenges posed by agriculture are huge, and they'll only become more pressing as we try to meet the growing need for food worldwide. We'll likely have 2 billion more mouths to feed by mid-century—more than 9 billion people. But sheer population growth isn't the only reason we'll need more food. The spread of **prosperity** across the world, especially in China and India, is driving an increased demand for meat, eggs, and dairy, boosting pressure to grow more corn and soybeans to feed more cattle, pigs, and chickens. If these trends continue, the double whammy of population growth and meat-and-dairy-intensive diets will require us to roughly double the amount of crops we grow by 2050.

3 I was fortunate to lead a team of scientists who confronted this simple question: How can the world double the availability of food while **simultaneously** cutting the environmental harm caused by agriculture? After analyzing reams of data on agriculture and the environment, we proposed five steps that could solve the world's food **dilemma**.

4 Taken together, these five steps could more than double the world's food supplies and dramatically cut the environmental impact of agriculture worldwide. But it won't be easy. These solutions require a big shift in thinking. For most of our history, we have been blinded by the imperative of more, more, more in agriculture—clearing more land, growing more crops, using more resources. We need to find a balance between producing more food and sustaining the planet for future generations.

STEP ONE: FREEZE AGRICULTURE'S FOOTPRINT

5 For most of history, whenever we've needed to produce more food, we've simply cut down forests or plowed grasslands to make more farms. We've already cleared an area roughly the size of South America to grow crops. To raise livestock, we've taken over even more land—an area roughly the size of Africa. Agriculture's footprint has caused the loss of whole ecosystems around the globe, including the prairies of North America and the Atlantic forest of Brazil, and tropical forests continue to be cleared at alarming rates. But we can no longer afford to increase food production through agricultural expansion. Trading tropical forest for farmland is one of the most destructive things we do to the environment, and it is rarely done to benefit the 850 million people in the world who are still hungry.

STEP TWO: GROW MORE ON FARMS WE'VE GOT

6 Starting in the 1960s, the green revolution increased **yields** in Asia and Latin America using better crop varieties and more fertilizer, irrigation, and machines—but with major environmental costs. The world can now turn its attention to increasing yields on less productive farmlands—especially in Africa, Latin America, and eastern Europe—where there are "yield gaps" between current production levels and those possible with improved farming practices. Using high-tech, precision farming systems, as well as approaches borrowed from organic farming, we could boost yields in these places several times over.

STEP THREE: USE RESOURCES MORE EFFICIENTLY

7 Organic farming can also greatly reduce the use of water and chemicals—by incorporating cover crops and compost to improve soil quality, conserve water, and build up nutrients. Many farmers have also gotten smarter about water, replacing **inefficient** irrigation systems with more **precise** methods, like subsurface drip irrigation. Advances in both conventional and organic farming can give us more "crop per drop" from our water and nutrients.

STEP FOUR: SHIFT DIETS

8 It would be far easier to feed 9 billion people by 2050 if more of the crops we grew ended up in human stomachs. Today only, 55 percent of the world's crop calories feed people directly; the rest are fed to livestock (about 36 percent) or turned into biofuels and industrial products (roughly 9 percent). Though many of us consume meat, dairy, and eggs from animals raised on feedlots, only a fraction of the calories in feed given to livestock make their way into the meat and milk that we consume. For every 100 calories of grain we feed animals, we get only about 40 new calories of milk, 22 calories of eggs, 12 of chicken, 10 of pork, or 3 of beef. Finding more efficient ways to grow meat and shifting to less meat-intensive diets—even just switching from grain-fed beef to meats like chicken, pork, or pasture-raised beef—could free up substantial amounts of food across the world.

STEP FIVE: REDUCE WASTE

9 An estimated 25 percent of the world's food calories and up to 50 percent of total food weight are lost or wasted before they can be consumed. In rich countries, most of that waste occurs in homes, restaurants, or supermarkets. In poor countries, food is often lost between the farmer and the market due to **unreliable** storage and transportation. Consumers in the developed world could reduce waste by taking such simple steps as serving smaller portions, eating leftovers, and encouraging cafeterias, restaurants, and supermarkets to develop waste-reducing measures. Of all of the options for boosting food availability, tackling waste would be one of the most effective.

Jonathan Foley directs the Institute on the Environment at the University of Minnesota.

---

compost: *n.* decaying organic material that is used as a plant fertilizer

subsurface drip irrigation: *n.* an underground watering system in which buried tubes provide small amounts of water directly to the roots of plants

Agriculture's Footprint

Farming of both livestock and crops is the largest human endeavor on Earth, using more than 38 percent of ice-free land. Our next largest impact: erosion caused by agriculture, building, logging, and mining.

> **"** We've already cleared an area roughly the size of South America to grow crops. **"**

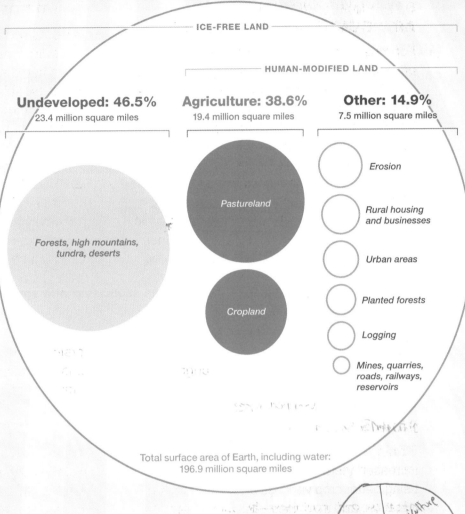

ICE-FREE LAND

HUMAN-MODIFIED LAND

Undeveloped: 46.5%
23.4 million square miles

Agriculture: 38.6%
19.4 million square miles

Other: 14.9%
7.5 million square miles

Forests, high mountains, tundra, deserts

Pastureland

Cropland

Erosion

Rural housing and businesses

Urban areas

Planted forests

Logging

Mines, quarries, roads, railways, reservoirs

Total surface area of Earth, including water: 196.9 million square miles

A World Demanding More

By 2050, the world's population will likely increase by about **35 percent.**

1 billion people

▲ 35%

To feed that population, crop production will need to **double.**

1 billion tons

▲ 100%

Why? Production will have to far outpace population growth as the developing world grows prosperous enough to eat more meat.

Developed countries — 15.3%

Increase in daily protein demand
Per capita by 2050

Developing countries — 103.6%

Least developed countries — 69.2%

GETTING THE MAIN IDEAS

Choose the best phrase to complete the overall main idea of the reading passage.

_____ may solve the problem of providing enough food for the world and reduce environmental stress at the same time.

1. Prosperity and a growing population

2. Changing diets and the way we approach agriculture

3. Investing in advanced technology for meat production.

UNDERSTANDING PROBLEMS

A. **Paragraph 1 explores some of the problems associated with agriculture. Complete the concept map below.**

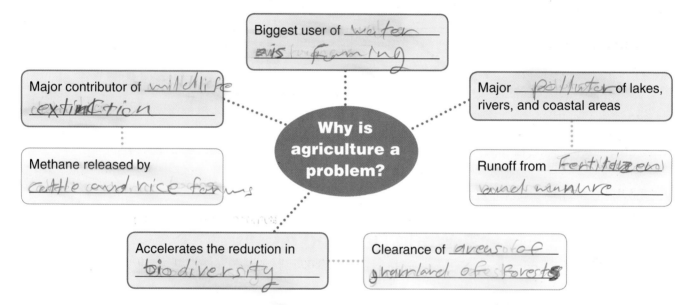

Biggest user of _water_ ans farming

Major contributor of _wildlife extinction_

Methane released by _cattle and rice farms_

Major _polluter_ of lakes, rivers, and coastal areas

Runoff from _Fertilizer and manure_

Why is agriculture a problem?

Accelerates the reduction in _biodiversity_

Clearance of _areas of grassland of forests_

B. **Use information from paragraph 2 and the infographic "A World Demanding More" on page 109 to summarize the environmental challenges posed by agriculture.**

1. We'll need to feed an additional ___a___ people by 2050.

   a. 2 billion   b. 7 billion   c. 9 billion

2. By 2050, rises in global wealth will ___a___.

   a. mean higher demand for meat, which requires more agricultural resources

   b. cause prices for crops to rise, which will result in much higher food prices

   c. lead to people worldwide eating more soybeans and corn products

3. Increased wealth and higher population mean we will need to ___c___ by 2050.

   a. double the number of farms

   b. eat twice as much food

   c. grow twice as many crops

IDENTIFYING SOLUTIONS

Complete the chart about each of Foley's proposed solutions. Use the ideas below.

a. crops

b. efficient

c. existing farms

d. expansion of farmland

e. limited resources like water

f. meat-based diets

g. rain forests and grasslands

h. storage and transportation

i. waste

j. yields

Step	Benefit
1. Stop _expansion of farmland_	Prevents destruction of _rain forest and grasslands_
2. Use new technologies to grow more on _existing farms_	Increases _yields_ on farms that are currently not very productive
3. Reduce use of _limited resources like water_	Makes farms more _b_
4. Move away from _meat-based diets_	Increases proportion of _h_ that feed people rather than animals
5. Improve food _crops_	Reduces _waste_

PARAPHRASING INFORMATION

Paraphrasing information—by restating, condensing, or clarifying an author's ideas—can help you to understand it better.

Use the information from the "Identifying Solutions" activity above to paraphrase each of Foley's steps.

Step 1: *The first step is to stop creating new farmland and instead use existing agricultural areas. This will prevent the destruction of rain forests and grasslands.*

Step 2: Use new technologies to grow more on existing farms.
Increases crops on farms that are currently not very productive

Step 3: Reduce use of limited resourses like water can make farms more efficient.

Step 4: Move away from meat-based diets. Increase proportion of storage and transportation that feed people rather than animals.

Step 5: Improve food yields. reduce waste.

UNDERSTANDING INFOGRAPHICS

Complete the following summary of the infographic "Agriculture's Footprint" on page 109.

The infographic shows that there is (less / ~~more~~) developed land than undeveloped land on the Earth's ice-free surface. In fact, only (38.6% / 46.5%) of ice-free land has not been altered by humans. The majority of developed land is used for (agriculture / urban areas). The land needed for pasture and crops is more than (double / half) the size of other human-modified land. The next largest impact on the land is (erosion / logging) caused by a variety of industries. While development of urban areas has had a significant impact on the world's surface, its impact on land use is (less / greater) than that of rural housing and businesses.

BUILDING VOCABULARY

A. Complete the paragraph with the words below. You may need to change the forms of the words.

emit	pose	prosper	simultaneously	yield

In "Feeding Nine Billion," Jonathan Foley points out that the appetite for meat is growing as the developing world enjoys greater _prosperity_ [1]. While increased wealth benefits everyone, eating more meat _poses_ [2] certain problems. For example, beef production, which _emits_ [3] about 18 percent of all greenhouse gases worldwide, is a significant contributor to climate change. Currently, global agreements to reduce greenhouse gases do not require countries to count emissions from agriculture in their emission-reduction plans. This is a benefit to nations that are just emerging from poverty. However, as Foley explains, all nations must take a hard look at the way they produce food. The reason is that increasing agricultural _yields_ [4] to feed a growing population could have a serious impact on the environment. The good news, though, is that there are several steps we can take right now to make food production more sustainable. Eating less meat is one way to accomplish this, while _simultaneously_ [5] adopting farming methods that are less stressful on the environment.

B. Complete the sentences with the correct definitions of the words in bold.

1. If you are in a **dilemma** about something, you are faced with a ____ between two alternatives.

   a. risk of choosing   b. difficult choice

2. If a method is more **precise**, it's ____.

   a. more common   b. more accurate

3. If a delivery system is **unreliable**, it's ____.

   a. not dependable   b. not healthy

4. If wealth **accelerates** meat consumption, it ____.

   a. causes it   b. speeds it up

5. If an agricultural system is **inefficient**, it does not ____.

   a. use resources in the best way   b. cost a lot of money to use

C. Choose the word that best collocates with each of the words in bold.

1. emit ____

   a. production   b. light   c. benefits

2. pose ____

   a. a danger   b. a plan   c. an impact

3. unreliable ____

   a. meat   b. population   c. service

4. inefficient ____

   a. use   b. cause   c. benefit

GETTING MEANING FROM CONTEXT

A. Find the phrases in bold in the passage. Then choose the meaning below that is the closest to the meaning in the passage.

1. Paragraph 1: **a major driver** (of something)

   a. a main result

   b. a significant cause

   c. a source of competition

2. Paragraph 4: **a big shift in thinking**

   a. a large improvement in understanding

   b. a great deal of hard work

   c. a major change in the way of viewing something

B. Complete the sentence with the correct phrase from Exercise A.

The food processing industry now accounts for 9 to 10 percent of India's GDP (Gross Domestic Product) and has become _a major driver_ of India's economic growth.

CRITICAL THINKING

Evaluating. Discuss these questions with a partner: Which of Foley's five steps do you think would be the hardest to achieve? Which would be the easiest? Why?

EXPLORE MORE

Read more about the future of food at nationalgeographic.com. Share what you learn with the class.

TEDTALKS

HOW FOOD SHAPES OUR CITIES

CAROLYN STEEL, Food urbanist, TED speaker

We can tell a lot about the historical role of food in people's lives by studying the history of cities. In her book, *Hungry City: How Food Shapes Our Lives*, British architect Carolyn Steel looks at how cities were organized around the ways that people produced food and then got it to their tables.

To illustrate this, Steel describes old London and shows how ancient food routes shaped the city of today. Street names like Bread Street and Poultry Street tell us a lot about what was happening in these parts of the city 300 years ago. In fact, she says, "If you were having Sunday lunch, the chances were it was mooing or bleating outside your window about three days earlier."

However, in the 20th century, Londoners—and other city dwellers—began driving their cars to suburban supermarkets to get their food, and as Steel points out, "This is the moment when our relationship, both with food and cities, changes completely." Steel feels that we are less connected today with our food and would like to reinvigorate the presence of food in cities. In her 2009 TED Talk, she proposes some ways to accomplish this.

---

dwellers: *n.* people who live in a place

reinvigorate: *v.* to make energetic or strong again

Carolyn Steel's **idea worth spreading** is that we really are what we eat. Food is a powerful tool that we should use to create the world we want to live in.

In this lesson, you are going to watch segments of Steel's TED Talk. Use the information about Steel on page 114 to answer each question.

1. What does Steel think we can learn by looking at how cities are organized?

   That we dont produce food in the cities
   Anymore is just this big metropolitan cities that people
   Just go to buy fast food and dont see natural food anymore

2. How can street names tell us about the food Londoners ate 300 years ago?

   They were eting corn, bread, meat and fish, most
   of the names of the citys before the industrial age was shared by the food

3. How is the modern relationship with food different, according to Steel?

   is That is not natural anymore we dont
   value food just throw it away because it's easy to
   buy more.

PART 1

AN ESCALATING PROBLEM

PREDICTING

In this segment of Carolyn Steel's talk, she discusses changes in food production and consumption. How do you think these areas will change between now and 2050? Complete the sentences and watch (▶) the segment to check your ideas.

1. About _____ of the world's annual grain crop goes to feeding animals instead of feeding people today.

   a. a quarter   **b.** a third   **c.** a half

2. The number of people living in cities could _____ by 2050.

   a. double   **b.** triple   **c.** quadruple

3. There will likely be _____ in the amount of meat we will be consuming in 2050.

   a. no change   **b.** a slight increase   **c.** a significant increase

4. Today, about _____ of all food produced in the U.S. is thrown away.

   a. 10 percent   **b.** 25 percent   **c.** 50 percent

UNDERSTANDING MAIN IDEAS

Choose three sentences that summarize Steel's main ideas in this segment.

_____ **1.** The process of feeding a large city is truly amazing, but we hardly ever think about it.

_____ **2.** Although most of us now live in cities, we are still dependent on the natural world.

_____ **3.** It has recently become very difficult to feed the entire population of London.

_____ **4.** Cities in the Western world are generally growing faster than in other parts of the world.

_____ **5.** As more people change to a meat-based diet, natural landscapes are being transformed.

CRITICAL THINKING

Inferring. Discuss your ideas with a partner.

Why does Steel show the photo of the soybean fields (see pages 104–105)? How does it support her main ideas?

ANALYZING ARGUMENTS

A. Analyze how Steel supports her argument that the Western diet is unsustainable. First, read the following excerpts and use the amounts to complete the missing numerical information.

billion   half   19 million   6 billion   ten   third   twice

❝ . . . a _third_ of the annual grain crop globally now gets fed to animals rather than to us human animals. And given that it takes _ten_ times as much grain—to feed a human if it's passed through an animal first, that's not a very efficient way of feeding us. ❞

❝ . . . By 2050, it's estimated that _twice_ ~~19 million~~ the number of us are going to be living in cities. And it's also estimated that there is going to be twice as much meat and dairy consumed. . . _6 billion_ hungry carnivores to feed, by 2050. That's a big problem. ❞

❝ . . . _19 million_ hectares of rain forest are lost every year to create new arable land. . . . _half_ the food produced in the U.S.A. is currently thrown away. . . .

A _a billion_ of us are obese, while a further billion starve. None of it makes very much sense. ❞

---

hectares: *n.* units of measure equal to 2.471 acres or 10,000 square meters

arable: *adj.* fit for farming

B. Compare the ideas in Foley's essay in Lesson A with those in Steel's talk. Note your answers and then discuss the questions with a partner.

1. What information in Steel's talk supports the ideas in Foley's essay?

_____

2. What ideas would each person agree on?

_____

3. In what ways are their arguments different?

→ Stop cutting forests

→ Increasing the yields in many crops

PART 2

RECONNECTING WITH FOOD

UNDERSTANDING MAIN AND SUPPORTING IDEAS

A. **In the next part of her talk Steel compares our relationship to food now and in the past. Read the excerpt below, and predict the missing words or phrases. Then watch (▶) the next segment to check your ideas.**

“ Here we have food—that used to be the <u>central</u>, the social core of the city—at

the periphery. It used to be a social event, buying and _____ food. Now it's

anonymous. We used to cook; now we just add _____, or a little bit of an egg if

you're making a cake . . . We don't _____ food to see if it's OK to eat. We just

read the back of a label on a packet. And we don't value food. . . . And instead of valuing

it, we ~~throw it~~ _____ away. »

B. **Steel makes the case for a new type of society, which she calls *Sitopia*. What characteristics of Sitopia does she mention? Check (✔) five characteristics.**

___ Food is at the center of family life.

___ It's based around independent city-states.

___ People take time for food, and celebrate it.

___ Markets sell food that is fresh and grown locally.

___ There are few supermarkets.

___ Community projects educate children about food.

___ Cities and nature are seen as part of the same framework.

C. **Can you think of any examples of Sitopia in your own city or town? Share your ideas with a partner.**

EXPLORE MORE

Find out more about how food shapes cities. Watch Steel's full talk at TED.com. How did ancient Rome feed its citizens? Share what you learn with the class.

Project

Chef and author Nick Saul in the Green Barn—a food community center he built where residents can grow, buy, and eat their own food in Toronto, Canada.

A. **Work with a partner. You are going to propose ways that people in your area can create a Sitopia.**

1. Go to TED.com and get some ideas from the following TED Talks.

   - Ron Finley, "A guerilla gardener in South Central L.A."
   - Pam Warhurst, "How we can eat our landscapes"
   - Britta Riley, "A garden in my apartment"
   - Roger Doiron, "My subversive (garden) plot"
   - Mark Bittman, "What's wrong with what we eat"

2. With your partner, answer these questions.

   - What types of food-related activities are realistic for your area? Consider weather, available space, the interests of the people in your community, and so on.
   - What are some possible locations for these activities?
   - How will these activities help people in your community reconnect with food?
   - How will these activities help the environment?
   - What other benefits will these activities have?

B. **Use your information to create a two-minute presentation on your proposal. You can use maps, photos, and video to explain your information.**

C. **Work with two other pairs.**

   - Present your proposals.
   - As you listen, take notes.
   - At the end, review your notes.
   - Have a class discussion. Which activities are the most realistic? Which have the most benefits? Do you have any suggestions for improving your classmates' proposals?

EXPLORE MORE

Learn more about how people in your community are changing their relationships with food. Has access to fresh food improved in recent years? Are there any signs of urban agriculture? Share what you learn with the class.

Robots move shelves of products through a warehouse in Arkansas, U.S.A. Demand for these robotic warehouse workers has surged in recent years as more retailers open huge distribution centers.

FUTURE
JOBS

GOALS

IN THIS UNIT, YOU WILL:

- Read about how technology might affect certain jobs.
- Learn about the new "machine age."
- Explore when and how certain jobs might become automated.

THINK AND DISCUSS

1. What jobs do you think might be replaced by robots and computers in the next ten years?

2. What makes those jobs particularly likely to become automated?

PRE-READING

A. What do you think robots and computers can do more efficiently than human beings? What are some things they can't do? Note your ideas and discuss with a partner.

•servers •cashiers
•driver •factory workers

B. Read the title and the headings of the reading. What aspects of cooking might a computer chef be better at than a human chef? What might a human chef be better at? Complete the chart with your ideas.

Computer chef is better at . . .

Human chef is better at . . .

C. Look at the final section heading. What do you think the word *obsolete* means? How can machines make us obsolete?

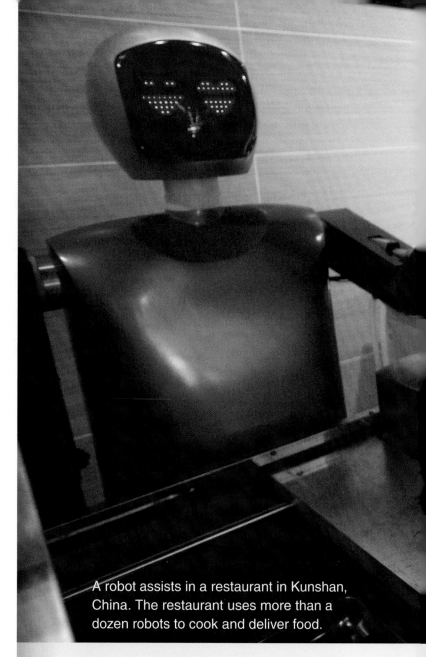

A robot assists in a restaurant in Kunshan, China. The restaurant uses more than a dozen robots to cook and deliver food.

BY REBECCA RUPP, National Geographic

1 Ever since the first mechanical computing machine was invented in the early 1800s, computers, it seems, have been creeping up on us.

2 A landmark event in the evolution of computers occurred in 2011, when an IBM supercomputer called Watson defeated all-time champ Ken Jennings at the TV quiz *Jeopardy*. Watson successfully answered difficult questions about the Beatles, the Olympics, Harry Potter, and Dracula—winning a prize worth $3.25 million.

RECIPES FOR INNOVATION

THINKING LIKE A HUMAN, BUT BETTER

3 Watson's specialty is answering questions—but unlike Google or Bing, it doesn't simply spit out a long list of links and expect users to dig out the solution for themselves. Instead, Watson delves into its immense digital database, using multiple algorithms to analyze a question in hundreds of different ways, generating hundreds of possible solutions. It then ranks these in order of probability to come up with—if not the one single correct answer—at least the best possible educated guess. Scientists refer to Watson's *modus operandi* as cognitive computing. Watson, in other words, may think somewhat like a human brain.

4 And now Watson—with hands-on help from chefs at the Institute of Culinary Education (ICE) in New York—is tackling cognitive cooking.

SHRIMP AND LICORICE? CAVIAR AND WHITE CHOCOLATE?

5 Generating a new recipe—it turns out—is no simple feat. Given the number of available ingredients and flavors, there are easily a

Customers in Austin, Texas, line up outside a food truck to buy items based on recipes created by Watson, IBM's cognitive computer.

quintillion—that's a one with 18 zeroes after it—different ways in which to put foods together in a dish, and no human cook can possibly evaluate them all. Watson's huge memory bank and lightning speed, however, are more than equal to the task—and it turns out that Watson can be creative, too.

6 Watson's cooking expertise draws on three different databases. It begins with its library of some 35,000 recipes, which collectively provide basic information about typical flavor combinations. This allows Watson to **deduce** the answer to questions such as "What ingredients are usually in a quiche?" It also knows the molecular chemistry of over 1,000 different ingredients—everything from black tea to Bantu beer. Finally, it has input from a field called "hedonic psychophysics," which quantifies how people respond to the chemical combinations that create flavor. In this case, the focus is on what people tend to like. (Shrimp and licorice? Caviar and white chocolate? Blue cheese and rum?) Watson's **mission**, based on these data, is to invent recipes that are both delicious and **unconventional**. And it looks like it's succeeding.

7 Given a **theme** and a description—say, "Spanish" and "breakfast bun," or "Thai" and "sweet potato"—Watson can come up with any number of suggestions, with lists of **novel** ingredients. Its culinary mix-and-matches have produced such unexpected combinations as bearmeat with saffron and sandalwood, and an off-the-wall kebab featuring 12 ingredients including pork, strawberries, curry, and mint. Other Watson inventions include Creole Shrimp-Lamb Dumpling, Baltic Apple Pie, Austrian Chocolate Burrito, and Bengali Butternut BBQ Sauce.

THE POTENTIAL OF COGNITIVE COMPUTING

8 Watson's supporters also see cognitive cooking as an opportunity to promote healthy eating—by coming up with inventive recipes that are low in fats and sugars, or specifically targeted at the diabetic, the lactose-intolerant, or others with special dietary needs. Perhaps, with Watson in their corner, school lunch providers will be inspired to move away from chicken fingers and hot dogs.

9 The proposed possibilities for cognitive computing are considerable, extending to any field that requires rapid analyses of large and

complex amounts of data. Watson may find a **niche**, for example, in the healthcare system, helping to diagnose patients, or predicting new and effective drugs; or in the sales and travel industries, analyzing massive amounts of data and predicting trends. It may even eventually be able to help you find a job.

ARE MACHINES MAKING US OBSOLETE?

10 In our computer-dominated world, it can make us nervous to consider our own clumsy **capabilities**. Is there anything we're good at that computers aren't better at? Are machines making us **obsolete**? Are our hard drives secretly laughing at us up their electronic sleeves? According to researchers, there still are a few skills in which humans **retain** superiority over computers. We're better at pattern recognition. We are capable of

emotional connections. We're more innovative. We tell better stories. And we're better at non-**routine** physical tasks such as gardening, portrait painting, and cabinet making—and, of course, cooking, which is why Watson leaves the real in-the-kitchen work to a team of trained chefs.

11 In the realm of food, however, people have one magnificent advantage over even the biggest and brightest of electronic brains. Computers may be brilliant when it comes to designing recipes. But people can eat.

---

algorithm: *n.* a process or set of rules to be followed in calculations

culinary: *adj.* related to cooking

diabetic: *n.* a person with diabetes, a disease in which there is too much sugar in the blood

lactose-intolerant: *n.* a person unable to digest milk products

modus operandi: *n.* a way of doing something

FUTURE JOBS AT RISK?

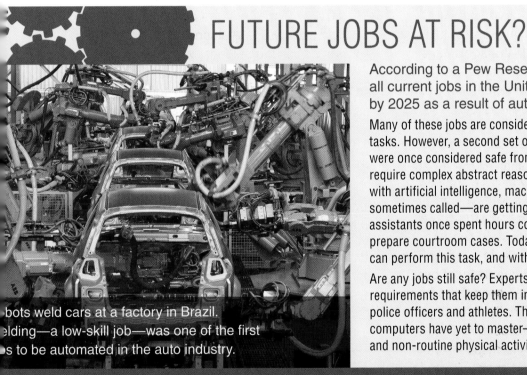

Robots weld cars at a factory in Brazil. Welding—a low-skill job—was one of the first jobs to be automated in the auto industry.

According to a Pew Research report, almost half of all current jobs in the United States could disappear by 2025 as a result of automation.

Many of these jobs are considered low-skill and involve routine tasks. However, a second set of jobs is also vulnerable. They were once considered safe from automation because they require complex abstract reasoning and judgment. But armed with artificial intelligence, machines—or droids as they are sometimes called—are getting smarter. For example, legal assistants once spent hours combing through documents to prepare courtroom cases. Today, however, machines like Watson can perform this task, and with greater speed and efficiency.

Are any jobs still safe? Experts suggest that some jobs have requirements that keep them in the "humans-only" zone, such as police officers and athletes. These kinds of jobs involve skills computers have yet to master—creativity, social intelligence, and non-routine physical activity.

Automated Jobs by 2025

low risk ➡ high risk

teachers	legal assistants	bank tellers
police	truck drivers	cashiers
actors	investment advisors	typists
professional athletes	researchers	proofreaders

125

Watson defeated its human challengers on the TV quiz show *Jeopardy* in 2011.

UNDERSTANDING ORGANIZATION AND PURPOSE

All texts have an overall purpose. In addition, different parts of a text may have different purposes, for example, to describe a process, compare things, explain a complex idea, provide a history, or tell a story. Identifying the purpose of different parts of a reading passage can help you understand the main ideas.

A. What is the overall purpose of the text? Choose the best statement.

1. To prove that computers are capable of doing the job of a chef

2. To demonstrate the power of computers to analyze massive amounts of data

3. To show that some computers' abilities are approaching human abilities

B. What is the purpose of each section of the passage? Match a purpose (a–g) to each section. There are more purposes than you will need.

Section 1 (paragraphs 1–2) _d_

Section 2 (paragraphs 3–4) _c_

Section 3 (paragraphs 5–7) _g_

Section 4 (paragraphs 8–9) _a_

Section 5 (paragraphs 10–11) _f_

a. to predict other possible uses of Watson's computing power

b. to describe the people behind Watson and how the program was developed

c. to explain cognitive computing and compare it to human cognition

d. to give a brief history of the competition between computers and humans

e. to describe some of the problems that cognitive computing can cause

f. to contrast human capabilities with those of advanced computers

g. to describe how Watson uses cognitive computing to generate recipes

CONNECTING PURPOSE TO MAIN IDEAS

Write the main idea for each section of the passage. Share your ideas with a partner.

Section 1: *In recent years, computers are becoming more and more powerful.*

Section 2: *Similar to humans, Watson's mind works by . . .* answering questions

Section 3: *Watson creates . . .*

Section 4: *In the future, . . .*

Section 5:

UNDERSTANDING KEY DETAILS

A. **What is Watson's purpose when creating new recipes? Underline the sentence or sentences that tell you (paragraph 6).**

B. **Complete the notes below to describe the sources of information that Watson uses to create a new recipe.**

> ### HOW WATSON CREATES A RECIPE
>
> • Has a library of _____. Provides information about
>
>   common _____.
>
> • Knows the chemical structure of _____.
>
> • Gets input from a field called hedonic psychophysics. Quantifies how people
>
>   react to _____.

C. **Look back at your answers to B on page 122. Did the reading raise any additional aspects of cooking that a computer chef can do better than a human chef? Add them to the chart.**

UNDERSTANDING A MAIN MESSAGE

A. Study the sections "Are Machines Making Us Obsolete?" and "Future Jobs at Risk" on page 125. Then complete the statements below.

1. Almost half of all jobs in the U.S.A. might be obsolete by 2025 because

   of _____, for example _____ and _____.

2. Complex tasks like reasoning and judgment can now be automated because

   computers work with more _____ and _____ than humans.

3. Jobs involving non-routine tasks are at _____ of automation by 2025.

B. Note answers to these questions and discuss with a partner.

1. According to the passage, what skills do humans have that are still superior to computers?

   _____

2. Do you agree with this list? Are there any other skills you would add to the list?

C. Do you think chefs are at high or low risk of automation by 2025? Why? Discuss the questions below with a partner.

BUILDING VOCABULARY

A. Complete the paragraph with the words below.

| capabilities | deduce | mission | obsolete | routine |

We rely on technology for all kinds of information and to perform _routine_ tasks:
1

What was that phone number? Where can I find some fish tacos? When Siri, the digital

assistant that responds to your voice, was introduced by Apple to the iPhone in 2012,

getting fast answers to questions like these became much easier. Like Siri, Watson is an

intelligent computer system that can also understand natural language. However, it has

more _capabilities_ because it also has access to a huge amount of specialized data.
2

Its _mission_ is to sift through vast amounts of data and _deduce_ patterns and
3   4

relationships. At the moment, Siri and Watson are owned by competing companies.

But what would happen if they were working together? Will they make human decision-

makers _obsolete_? Only time will tell.
5

B. **Find these bolded words in the reading passage. Match each one with the correct definition.**

1. **niche** _e_
2. **novel** _b_
3. **retain** _d_
4. **theme** _a_
5. **unconventional** _c_

a. overall topic
b. new and original
c. outside common practice; different
d. to keep, continue to have
e. a special place or position

C. **Underline the two words that best collocate with each of the words in bold.**

1. **niche** _a/b_   a. market   b. product   c. manager
2. _b/c_ **theme**   a. middle   b. common   c. underlying
3. _a/b_ **a mission**   a. complete   b. carry out   c. put out
4. _a/c_ **routine**   a. daily   b. fine   c. normal

GETTING MEANING FROM CONTEXT

Review how each phrase in bold is used. Circle the word or phrase that is closest in meaning to the phrase.

1. We need to **come up with** a plan by tomorrow.

   a. revise   b. think of   c. move on

2. He is a very **hands-on** manager.

   a. touchy   b. involved   c. physically active

3. It was not clear which members of the group were really **in our corner**.

   a. honest with us   b. stuck   c. supporting us

4. I have a really **off-the-wall** idea, but I would like you to listen to it.

   a. unpopular   b. unconventional   c. complicated

CRITICAL THINKING

Predicting. The passage suggests that computers like Watson will perform a substantial number of jobs within the near future. What might be the positive and negative effects of this? Discuss with a partner.

EXPLORE MORE

Find out more about cognitive cooking. Go online and search for "Cognitive cooking recipes." What recipes do you think are the most unusual? Which ones would you like to try? Share your ideas with your class.

TEDTALKS

WHAT WILL FUTURE JOBS LOOK LIKE?

ANDREW McAFEE Management theorist, TED speaker

Andrew McAfee is convinced that modern information technology (I.T.) is the most powerful resource available to business and government leaders today. Yet he says it is also the most misunderstood and underappreciated.

McAfee—a research scientist at the Center for Digital Business at the MIT Sloan School of Management—studies the ways that information technology affects business and the larger society. His research investigates how technology changes the way companies perform, organize themselves, and compete, and how computerization affects society, the economy, and the workforce.

According to McAfee, I.T. will have a significant and not necessarily positive impact on the economy and the workforce in the near future. Artificial intelligence, sophisticated algorithms, and access to massive data allow intelligent machines to do complex work—like diagnosing a patient's symptoms. As a result, McAfee says, even doctors are vulnerable to coming changes.

---

vulnerable: *adj.* easily attacked or harmed

Andrew McAfee's **idea worth spreading** is that as droids take over many of the jobs humans do now, we'll have to come up with innovative ways to ensure that everyone has the education and income they need to thrive.

In this lesson, you are going to watch segments of McAfee's TED Talk. Use the information about McAfee on page 130 to answer the questions below.

1. What is the focus of McAfee's research?

    the way that information tecnology affects business and the larger society.

2. What makes modern information technology particularly powerful?

    artificial intelligence, sophisticated algorithms, and access to massive data allow intelligence machines to do complex work

3. How could I.T. affect a doctor's job?

    _____

TEDTALKS

PART 1

THE NEW MACHINE AGE

PREVIEWING

Read the excerpt from Andrew McAfee's talk. What do you think he means? Can you think of any examples? Discuss with a partner.

> « In the world that we are creating very quickly, we're going to see more and more things that look like science fiction, and fewer and fewer things that look like jobs. »

GETTING THE MAIN IDEAS

Watch (▶) the first segment of McAfee's talk. Choose the sentence that best describes the "new machine age" according to McAfee.

a. Technology will take over many of the jobs we currently have.

b. As robots become more efficient, there will be fewer of them.

c. Machines will do the jobs we are not able to do.

PART 2

NEW POSSIBILITIES

PREVIEWING AND PREDICTING

Read the excerpt below from McAfee's talk and then answer the questions with a partner. Check your ideas as you watch (▶) the next part of the talk.

> « The people who used to be craftsmen and hobbyists are now makers, and they're responsible for massive amounts of innovation. And artists who were formerly constrained can now do things that were never, ever possible for them before. »

1. Based on this excerpt, is McAfee hopeful about the future? Yes

2. What types of jobs especially benefit from the new machine age?
   Creativity.

3. Why do you think these jobs might be important?
   Because this jobs about create thing with our own hand cant be replaced.

CRITICAL THINKING

Predicting. McAfee ends this segment by asking, "What could possibly go wrong in this new machine age?" Discuss possible answers with a classmate.

PART 3

BILL AND TED

IDENTIFYING TRENDS

A. In the next segment, McAfee introduces two stereotypical characters—Bill and Ted—who represent different parts of society. Look at the graphs below. How have the lives of people like Bill and Ted changed in the last 40 years? Discuss with a partner.

families in which the head of household or spouse worked 40 or more hours in the preceding week

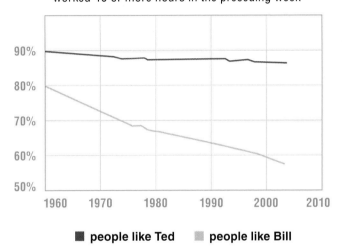

■ people like Ted   ■ people like Bill

proportion of all whites ages 30–49 who self-report being in very happy marriages

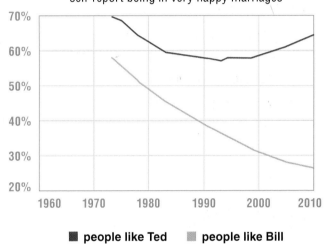

■ people like Ted   ■ people like Bill

Source: Charles Murray, *Coming Apart*

B. What kinds of workers do you think Bill and Ted are? Match a name to each description. Then watch (▶) the next segment to check your ideas.

Ted college educated; manager, doctor, lawyer, engineer, scientist, professor, content producer

Bill no college education; blue-collar worker (e.g., factory), low-level admin or service worker

C. Which type of person does each statement describe, Bill or Ted? Use information from McAfee's talk, and the graphs above, to complete each statement.

1. More than 80% of people like _Ted_ work 40 hours or more each week, although the number has fallen slightly.

2. People like _Bill_ have seen a sharp decline in the happiness of their marriages.

3. The children of people like _ted_ mostly grow up in a two-parent home; this hasn't changed much since 1960.

4. The percentage of people like _Bill_ voting in presidential elections has fallen by about 20%.

5. There is a much higher proportion of people like _Bill_ in prison than just a few decades ago.

PART 4

SO WHAT DO WE DO?

UNDERSTANDING SOLUTIONS

A. **McAfee outlines some ways for us to prepare for the future. Watch (▶) the next segment of his talk, and choose the four economic solutions he proposes.**

_____ **1.** Lower the cost of education.

__✓__ **2.** Encourage entrepreneurship.

__✓__ **3.** Improve infrastructure.

__✓__ **4.** Ensure that students learn appropriate skills.

_____ **5.** Reduce taxes for poorer people.

__✓__ **6.** Introduce a minimum income.

B. **Read the excerpt below. Then answer the questions with a partner.**

❝ With the benefit of hindsight, I now know the job [of public school] was to prepare me for life as a clerk or a laborer, but at the time it felt like the job was to kind of bore me into some submission with what was going on around me. We have to do better than this. We cannot keep turning out Bills. ❞

1. What does McAfee mean when he says "we cannot keep turning out Bills"? Why does McAfee feel this way? Discuss your ideas with a partner.

2. What does McAfee say about societal solutions in this segment? Choose two options.

    (a.) He's not really sure what the solutions are.

    b. He argues that all kids should go to a Montessori school.

    c. He thinks we should improve training for manual workers.

    (d.) He thinks better education might help.

CRITICAL THINKING

Personalizing. Do you feel as hopeful about the "new machine age" as McAfee? Why or why not?

EXPLORE MORE

Watch McAfee's full TED Talk at TED.com. Find out more about McAfee's ideas on how to prepare for the new machine age. Share what you learned with your classmates.

Project

A customer uses an automated self-checkout in a supermarket in Baden, Switzerland.

A. **Work in a small group. You are going to prepare a poster about when and how jobs could become automated. Follow the steps below.**

1. Look at the list of jobs. Research any you don't know about.

Architect	Fiction writer
Airline pilot	Politician
Eye doctor	TV sports commentator

2. In your groups, discuss the following questions.

   • Do you think each job could become automated? Think about the kinds of skills involved with each job.
   • In what order do you think these jobs could be automated?
   • What aspects of each job do you think could become automated?

B. **Prepare a poster summarizing your group's discussion. Include the following items on your poster.**

   • Pictures of some of the jobs
   • An estimate of when each job might become automated
   • A short description of how each job might become automated

C. **Present your poster to the class. After each group has presented, discuss the similarities and differences between the posters.**

EXPLORE MORE

Learn more about the future of work. Read the TED Blog post "The future of work and innovation" at TED.com. Share your information with the class.

HOW WE LEARN

Melodie George-Moore at her home with her daughter in Hoopa, California, U.S.A. Discouraged from speaking Hupa, her native language, when she was a child, Melodie works to help future generations learn the language.

GOALS

IN THIS UNIT, YOU WILL:

- Read about research on language learning and the brain.
- Learn how babies' brains change as they grow.
- Explore more about raising bilingual children.

THINK AND DISCUSS

1. At what age did you begin studying a second language? Why did you start learning the language?

2. What have been some of your greatest challenges in learning a second language?

PRE-READING

A. **Study the graph on page 140 and answer the questions with a partner.**

1. According to the graph, at what time in our lives are we best at learning a language?

   _____

2. What happens to our ability to learn language as we become adults?

   _____

3. What do you think might be responsible for this change?

   _____

B. **Read the title of the passage and then answer the questions below. Check your answers later when you read the passage.**

1. How do you think researchers are able to study language learning in babies that are still too young to speak?

   _____

   _____

   _____

2. What kinds of language abilities do babies have? Discuss with a partner.

   _____

   _____

   _____

Julien Inzodda teaches her daughter about spices in her kitchen in Pittsburgh, Pennsylvania, U.S.A. It's a playful opportunity for the toddler to learn words to describe color, texture, and taste.

🔊 We prefer people who speak the same way we do. Current research suggests that this preference is hard-wired and emerges at a very young age in a variety of subtle ways.

1   Most of us can easily distinguish between spoken English and French. But could you tell the difference between an English and a French speaker based only on visual clues—just by looking at the movements of their lips? This seems a difficult task for most adults. But surprising new evidence suggests that babies can meet this challenge at just a few months of age.

WHAT BABIES KNOW ABOUT LANGUAGE AND WHY WE SHOULD CARE

ED YONG, Phenomena blog, National Geographic

2 Research has shown that even young infants can tell the difference between the sounds of different languages. Psychologist Whitney Weikum and researchers from the University of British Columbia decided to develop this research by testing babies' powers of visual **discrimination**.

3 In the experiment, the researchers showed babies from English-speaking families silent video clips. The clips showed bilingual French-English speakers reading out the same sentence in one of the two languages. Each baby watched the faces of the speakers without hearing the words.

4 When the babies had become **accustomed to** these, Weikum showed them different clips of the same speakers reading out a new sentence. In some cases, the sentence was in the same language as before; in other cases, the sentence was in the other language.

5 When the language was switched, the babies spent more time looking at the speaker on their screen. This is a standard test used by child psychologists, and it means that the infants saw something that drew their attention. They had noticed the language change, based only on lip movement.

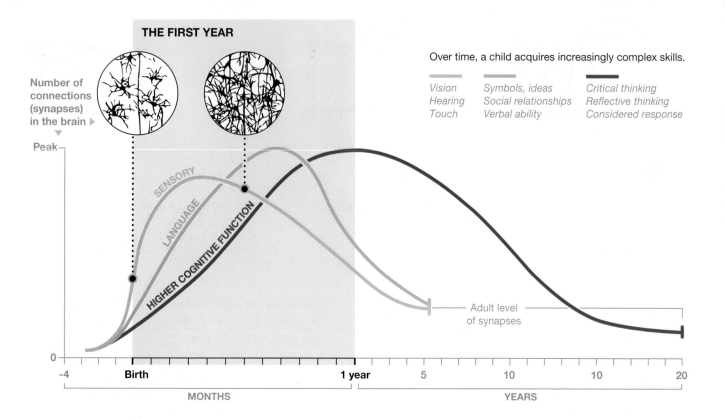

THE FIRST YEAR

Number of connections (synapses) in the brain ▶

Peak—

Over time, a child acquires increasingly complex skills.

Vision | Symbols, ideas | Critical thinking
Hearing | Social relationships | Reflective thinking
Touch | Verbal ability | Considered response

SENSORY

LANGUAGE

HIGHER COGNITIVE FUNCTION

Adult level of synapses

0—

-4   Birth   1 year   5   10   10   20

MONTHS   YEARS

A CRITICAL AGE?

6 So why can't you do what these babies can accomplish so easily? The research showed that the babies have this ability at four to six months of age, but lose it by their eighth month. Other studies have yielded similar findings—during the same period, infants begin to lose their ability to discriminate among the sounds of unfamiliar languages. It seems that infants are **initially** sensitive to the properties of a wide range of languages. But without continued exposure, their sensitivities soon narrow to the range that is most relevant for their own language. To test this idea, Weikum and her colleagues repeated the experiments with infants from bilingual homes. Sure enough, at eight months these babies could still visually tell the difference between English and French speakers.

EARLY PREFERENCES SET THE STAGE

7 This research shows that as babies grow, they remain sensitive to the details of their own language but not of other languages. This sensitivity is important for the essential task of language learning. However, this preference for our own language over others has another important effect—babies also prefer speakers

of their mother tongue from a very early age. In other words, they have a preference for particular people—as well as particular sounds. Katherine Kinzler and her colleagues from Harvard University have found that babies develop these preferences long before they can speak.

8 To investigate this idea of early linguistic preference, Kinzler tested infants (aged five to six months) from households that only spoke English. Each baby watched videos of two bilingual women, one speaking English and the other Spanish. The babies then watched the women on two screens at the same time, but no longer speaking. The babies expressed their preference for the woman who had spoken English by looking at that screen for a longer time.

LINGUISTIC PREFERENCE OR LINGUISTIC PREJUDICE?

9 Our preference for speakers of our own language offers a clear evolutionary advantage. It provides babies with exposure to the language they need to learn and allows them to distinguish between members of their own group, and outsiders. But are there other social, cultural, and perhaps even political

In Kinzler's experiment, a baby from an English-speaking family watches and listens to a woman saying something in English.

The baby then watches a different woman saying something in Spanish.

The baby then watches both women on two screens at the same time, but with the sound off. In most cases, the baby looks longer at the woman who had spoken English.

consequences of this preference for speakers of our own language? Is there a **downside** to this remarkable ability?

10 It is clear from the research of scientists like Weikum and Kinzler that we form linguistic preferences very early—well before we can understand the social issues at stake. But these preferences also have the potential to foster prejudice, or even destructive behavior, later on in life. Linguistic differences can drive us apart and act as massive **barriers** between different social groups. Language-based prejudice has led to terrible acts of **abuse**, and even civil wars (see the "Banned Languages" section below). Even today, people in linguistic minorities may be denied access to resources, and are often at a disadvantage when looking for jobs.

11 Although the biological origins of linguistic prejudice have been demonstrated by a growing body of research, we must be very careful—an **instinctive** basis for a behavior does not in any way **justify** it. Instead, by telling us about the basis of linguistic prejudice, this research suggests that we must work even harder to overcome it. If our linguistic preferences are hardwired from an early age, then early education—perhaps including exposure to multiple languages—seems like a sensible first step.

---

civil war: *n.* a war between opposing groups from the same country

boarding school: *n.* a school where young students live as well as study

mother tongue: *n.* the first language one learns as a child

property: *n.* quality; characteristic

suppression: *n.* the prevention of an activity from continuing

BANNED LANGUAGES

One way to erase a community's identity and power is to **eliminate** its language. **Banning** the use of minority languages in schools and other public places has a long history. For example, the minority language Catalan was banned in Spain during the mid-20th century, as were national languages in many eastern European republics during the Soviet period, after Russian became the official language.

Some of the worst modern abuses occurred in the United States during the 19th and early 20th centuries. Many Native American children were taken from their homes and educated in boarding schools, where they were punished if they spoke their mother tongue. By taking away their language, the government attempted to break the children's link to their own culture and force them to become part of American culture. Speakers of Hawaiian and native Australian languages suffered a similar fate during the same period.

In some cases, banned languages eventually disappeared. In other cases, however, languages that were once banned have been revived. Today, for example, the languages of the former Soviet Union are again used in schools and public places, and the vibrant Catalan language is a source of fierce pride among its speakers.

GETTING THE MAIN IDEAS

What is the reading passage mainly about? Check (✔) the best answer.

1. _____ Minority languages, such as Catalan, that are under threat

2. _____ Research about the advantages of bilingualism for children and adults

3. _✓_ Changes in linguistic ability and preference that occur at a very early age

UNDERSTANDING PURPOSE AND SEQUENCE

A. The passage includes information about two experiments. What did each researcher want to find out? Complete each sentence with the best option (a–d).

   a. whether babies prefer someone from one linguistic group over another

1. Weikum wanted to test _____.

   b. whether babies prefer listening to their parents' language rather than someone else's

2. Kinzler wanted to test _____.

   c. how well babies could see the difference between languages

   d. how soon babies could speak their native language

B. How did each experiment work? Complete each flow chart with the words and phrases (a–i).

   a. different
   b. bilingual
   c. English
   d. English-only
   e. English-speaking
   f. French or English
   g. heard
   h. silent
   i. speak

Weikum's Experiment

Involved babies from _e_ families

↓

Babies watched _h_ video clips of _b_ speakers reading a sentence

↓

Babies then watched silent clips of the same speakers reading new sentences in either _f_

↓

Babies noticed when speakers used a _a_ language

Kinzler's Experiment

Tested babies from _d_ homes

↓

A baby watched and _g_ bilingual women, one speaking English and the other Spanish

↓

The baby then looked at the speakers at the same time, but this time the women did not _i_

↓

Babies looked longer at the woman who had been speaking _c_

C. Use the phrases (a–f) to complete the summary of the two experiments.

a. another consequence   **c.** in their own language   **e.** speakers of our own language

b. of any language   **d.** linguistic prejudice   **f.** visual and sound cues

Babies are highly sensitive to ___f___ related to language. When they are four to
                                  1

six months, babies are sensitive to the properties ___b___, but by eight months,
                                                      2

they can only discriminate among these cues ___c___. This focus on our own
                                              3

language has ___a___: From a very early age, we prefer ___e___. This trait
             4   5

can sometimes lay the foundation for ___d___ later in life.
                                      6

APPLYING INFORMATION

Applying concepts that you have learned to a new situation can deepen your understanding of
an academic text.

**Based upon what you learned from the reading passage, do you think the following
activities are likely (*L*) or unlikely (*U*) for a baby raised in a French-speaking home?
Discuss your answers with a partner and explain your reasoning.**

The child . . .	5 months	10 months
1. can distinguish between the lip movements used for speaking English and French.		
2. can discriminate between the sounds of French.		
3. can discriminate between the sounds of English.		
4. will show preference for a French speaker.		
5. will show preference for an English speaker.		

BUILDING VOCABULARY

A.   Choose the best word to complete each sentence.

accustomed to   downside   initially   instinctive   justify

1. Research suggests that there really is no _downside_ to bilingualism. In school,
   bilingual children do just as well as children who speak only one language.

2. _Initially_, children can distinguish among the sounds of any language, but they
   soon lose this ability.

3. Babies stop responding to a sound when they become _accustomed to_ it.

4. Many language researchers believe that language learning is a type of _instinctive_
   behavior, one that is based in our genes.

5. Educators can use research results like these to _justify_ an investment in early
   language-learning classes.

B.   Match each word in bold to its definition.

1. abuse _c_

    a. something that keeps people or things apart

2. barrier _a_

    b. to be able to tell the difference between two or more things

3. eliminate _d_

    c. cruel treatment

4. ban _e_

    d. to remove or take away

5. discriminate _b_

    e. to say something cannot be done or used

C.   Discuss the following questions with a partner.

1. Do you think there is any *downside* to learning a new language? Explain your answer.

2. When language differences prevent communication, we often call this a *language barrier*. Have you been in a situation in which there was a language barrier? Describe it to your partner.

GETTING MEANING FROM CONTEXT

A.   Review how each phrase in bold is used in the reading passage. Then circle the word or phrase that is closest in meaning.

1. *If our linguistic preferences are **hardwired** from an early stage, then early education . . . seems like a sensible first step.* (Paragraph 11)

    Hardwired is an ability that is _____.

    a. difficult to understand

    b. fixed and cannot be changed

2. ***Sure enough,** at eight months these babies could still visually tell the difference between English and French speakers.* (Paragraph 6)

    You use **sure enough** to say something is _____.

    a. as expected

    b. very likely

3. *Even today, people in linguistic minorities may be denied access to resources, and are often **at a disadvantage** when looking for jobs.* (Paragraph 10)

    If you are **at a disadvantage**, you _____.

    a. have a difficulty other people don't have that makes it harder to succeed

    b. are in an unusual situation that makes others think badly of you

B.   Do you think people are at a disadvantage if they speak only their native language? Discuss your answer with a partner.

CRITICAL THINKING

Interpreting. Review the section "Banned Languages" on page 141. Then, with a partner, answer the questions below.

1. What acts of abuse does "Banned Languages" describe?

   _____

2. How might this abuse be related to linguistic prejudice?

   _____

   _____

3. In the main reading passage, the author warns that " . . . we must be very careful—an instinctive basis for a behavior does not in any way justify it." What does he mean?

   _____

   _____

EXPLORE MORE

Read more about the early cognitive development of babies and the power of language learning at ngm.nationalgeographic.com/2015/01/baby-brains/bhattacharjee-text. Share your information with the class.

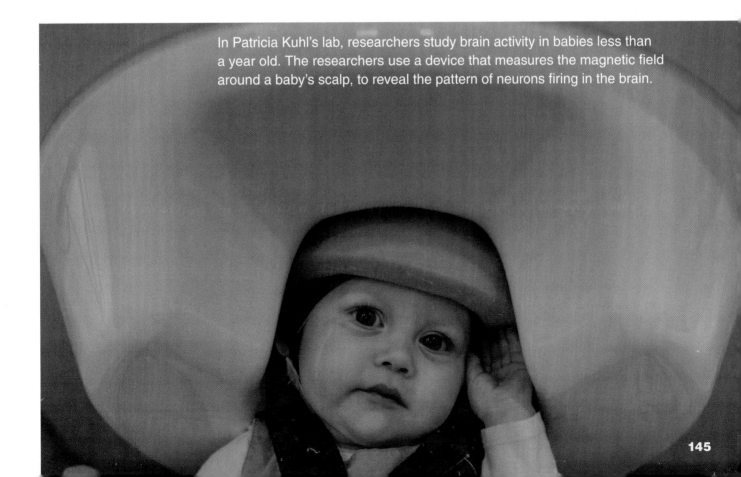

In Patricia Kuhl's lab, researchers study brain activity in babies less than a year old. The researchers use a device that measures the magnetic field around a baby's scalp, to reveal the pattern of neurons firing in the brain.

TEDTALKS

THE LINGUISTIC GENIUS OF BABIES

PATRICIA KUHL, Language researcher, TED speaker

🔊 "Babies and children are geniuses until they turn seven," says Patricia Kuhl, "and then there's a systematic decline."

Patricia Kuhl, co-director of the Institute for Brain and Learning Sciences at the University of Washington, is referring to babies' incredible capacity to absorb and learn languages. Just as incredibly, that capacity seems to disappear as they grow older. Scientists around the world are trying to figure out why this happens.

Kuhl's lab is one of those working on this puzzle. Kuhl—a leading authority on language development in babies and young children—studies how this development is reflected in the brain. Her work focuses on what have been called "critical periods" in development, particularly in language learning. Kuhl's work has important implications for education, automatic speech recognition, and our understanding of language disabilities.

---

genius: *n.* a person with extremely high intelligence

In this lesson, you are going to watch segments of Kuhl's TED Talk. Use the information about Kuhl above to answer each question.

1. What puzzle is Kuhl trying to solve?

   language development in babies a young children.

2. In what areas could Kuhl's research have an impact?

   has important implication for education, automatic speech recognition, and our understanding of language disabilities.

3. What is a "critical period"?

Patricia Kuhl's **idea worth spreading** is that babies have remarkably sophisticated innate reasoning that they use to process and understand language.

TEDTALKS

CITIZENS OF THE WORLD

PREVIEWING

Read this excerpt from Patricia Kuhl's talk. Why do you think she uses the phrase "rocket science" when talking about babies' brains? Discuss your answers with a partner.

❝ [T]oday I'm going to talk to you about something you can't see—what's going on up in that little brain of [the baby]. The modern tools of neuroscience are demonstrating to us that what's going on up there is nothing short of rocket science. ❞

nothing short of: *idiom* equal to; at least the same as

GETTING THE MAIN IDEAS

In the first part of her talk, Kuhl talks about her research. Watch (▶) the segment and complete the concept map of her main ideas.

PURPOSE
Kuhl looked at when babies try to master the _sounds_ that are used in their language.

METHODOLOGY
A baby is trained to turn his or her head when a sound _changes_. If the baby does so at the right _time_, a box lights up and a panda bear pounds a drum.

Kuhl's Research

RESULTS
Babies can discriminate among _all_ the sounds of any human language. But by the time children reach their _first_ birthday, they can discriminate only among the sounds of their own language.

CRITICAL THINKING

Interpreting. Discuss the questions with a partner.

1. Kuhl says that adults are "culture-bound" listeners. What does "culture-bound" mean?

2. How does being a culture-bound listener help or hinder us?

TAKING STATISTICS

UNDERSTANDING VISUALS

A. Look at the graphs from the next part of Kuhl's talk that show the results of her experiment. Note your answers to the questions below. Then watch (▶) the next segment of Kuhl's talk and check your ideas.

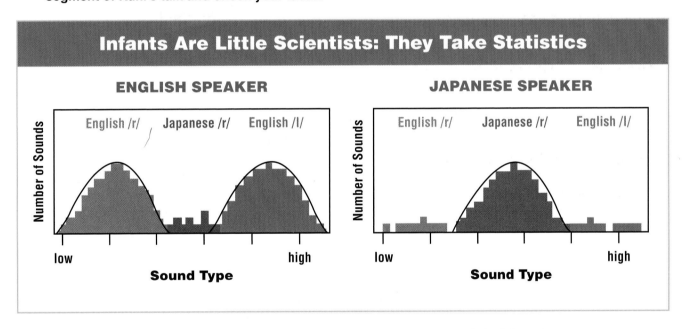

1. What do the graphs show about the differences between the sounds of English and the sounds of Japanese?

_____

_____

_____

2. How is this connected to Kuhl's research into language learning in babies?

_____

_____

B. **Complete the paragraph about Kuhl's conclusions during this part of her talk.**

At this critical age, babies take ___statistics___ on the sounds they hear,

which makes them become ___culture-bound___ listeners. In other words, they

hear best the sounds of the native language spoken around them.

RECOGNIZING TONE AND MESSAGE

Read the excerpt below from Kuhl's talk, and then answer the questions.

❝ We are embarking on a grand and golden age of knowledge about a child's brain development. We're going to be able to see a child's brain as they experience an emotion, as they learn to speak and read, as they solve a math problem, as they have an idea. And we're going to be able to invent brain-based interventions for children who have difficulty learning. Just as the poets and writers described, we're going to be able to see, I think, that wondrous openness, utter and complete openness, of the mind of a child. In investigating the child's brain, we're going to uncover deep truths about what it means to be human, and in the process, we may be able to help keep our own minds open to learning for our entire lives. ❯❯

1. Choose the statement that best matches Kuhl's overall message.

   a. It is important for all of us to remain citizens of the world and be open to new experiences.

   b. This research will help us understand how the brain works and could benefit both children and adults.

   c. This research will reveal how understanding language is related to other kinds of thinking processes.

2. Choose the best adjective below to describe Kuhl's tone. Which words and phrases from the excerpt helped you decide? Discuss with a partner.

   a. concerned

   b. optimistic

   c. cautious

CRITICAL THINKING

1. Evaluating. Which do you think was a more effective way of explaining the purpose and findings of this kind of research—the TED Talk or the reading passage in Lesson A? Discuss with a partner.

2. Synthesizing. What are the similarities between the "golden age of knowledge" that Kuhl talks about and the "golden age of exploration" Brian Cox discusses in Unit 1? Discuss with a partner.

EXPLORE MORE

Watch Patricia Kuhl's full talk at TED.com. Find out about other research being done in her lab.

Project

Kuna students learning vocabulary at a
Spanish-Kuna bilingual school in Panama.

A. **Work with a partner. Your class has been asked by an online magazine to write a blog post on the best tips for raising bilingual children.**

1. Research some of these issues so you can decide on your focus.

   - What is the best method when one or both parents' mother tongue is different from the language of the outside community?
   - What is the best method when both parents speak the language of the outside community as their mother tongue?
   - What kinds of activities outside of school help promote bilingualism?
   - How can parents create a network of bilingual friends for their child?

2. Create your blog post.

   - Include graphs or statistics if possible.
   - Include recommendations in your post.
   - Include evidence to support each recommendation.

B. **Read the other pairs' posts.**

   - Which suggestions seemed the most useful in each post?
   - Which ideas in the posts surprised you?

EXPLORE MORE

Find out more about the early stages of language learning. Watch Deb Roy's TED Talk "The birth of a word" at TED.com.

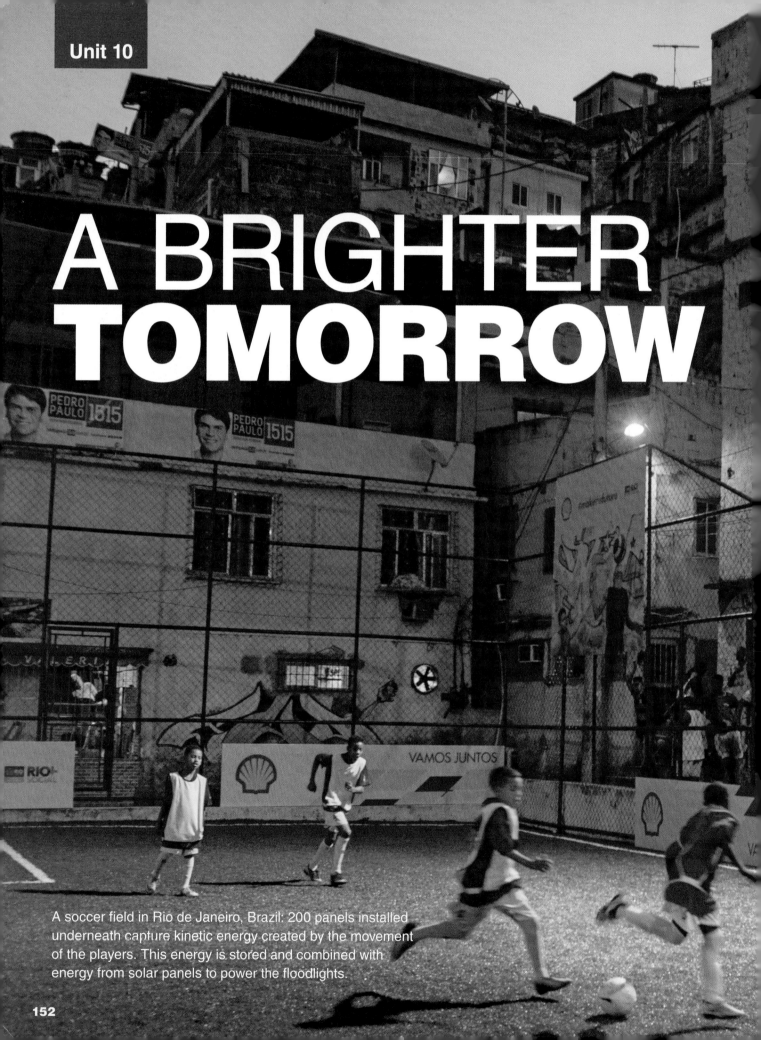

A BRIGHTER TOMORROW

A soccer field in Rio de Janeiro, Brazil: 200 panels installed underneath capture kinetic energy created by the movement of the players. This energy is stored and combined with energy from solar panels to power the floodlights.

GOALS

IN THIS UNIT, YOU WILL:

- Read about the global energy challenges we face.
- Learn about one man's vision for the future of energy.
- Explore ways you can reduce your energy usage.

THINK AND DISCUSS

1. What are the most common sources of energy in your country?

2. How are sources of energy changing? Which do you think are becoming more popular? Why?

PRE-READING

A. **Look at the photos and read the captions on pages 155 and 157. Then answer the questions below with a partner.**

1. What kinds of energy production does each photo show?

_____

_____

2. Complete the chart with some advantages and disadvantages of different forms of energy.

Fossil Fuels (e.g., oil)
Pros:
Cons:

Renewable Energy (e.g., wind)
Pros:
Cons:

B. **Read the introduction and first paragraph. What do you think you will read about? Note your answers and check your ideas as you read the passage.**

_____

_____

_____

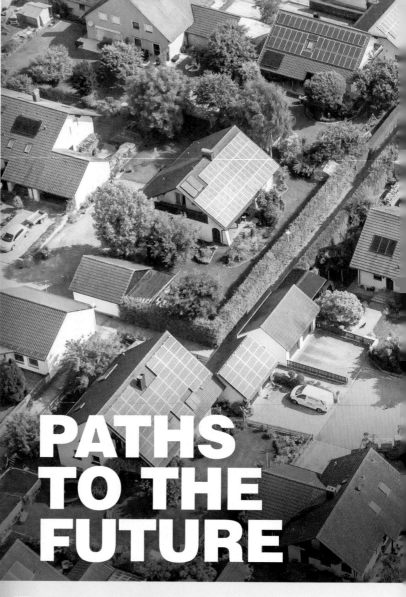

PATHS TO THE FUTURE

BILL McKIBBEN, National Geographic

Journalist turned environmental activist, Bill McKibben is the founder of 350.org, an organization that works to raise awareness of climate issues. In this essay, adapted from an article for *National Geographic*, McKibben outlines the challenges we must overcome to ensure a better energy future.

Newly constructed houses with photovoltaic solar roof panels in Sünching, Germany

1 I'm writing these words on a computer powered by the solar panels on the roof of my house—that's the good news. We're learning some new ways that we might power our lives. But *might* is the operative word. It's not going to be easy, and however well we manage the **transition** away from oil and coal and gas, the world we create won't be the same.

2 To understand why, consider the **intrinsic** merits of fossil fuel: It's easy to get at (just stick a drill in the ground, or, tragically, blow the top off a West Virginia mountain), easy to transport, and incredibly rich in power. One barrel of oil, for instance, contains about 5.8 million Btu, or the **equivalent** of the force exerted by a peasant working 3,625 hours on a farm. That would be, oh, about 15 months' worth of work in the fields. Fossil fuel is magical stuff.

3 Renewable energy, by contrast, is certainly plentiful. In any given hour, more energy from the sun reaches Earth than is used by the whole human population in any given year. The trouble, of course, is that it's the very opposite of coal or oil. Instead of being **concentrated**, it's diffused. There's a little bit everywhere, except at night, when there isn't any at all. The same with wind and with many other **alternatives**.

4 This doesn't necessarily make them impractical. While there are no simple solutions, we're not completely without hope. Still, it's very hard to see quite how we'll power the world we're used to living in. Look at the whole apparatus of our society as you head to work or school today: the thrumming of the engine in your car, the whir of the machine that makes your coffee (not to mention the

155

ship that carries the coffee to our shores and the roaster that makes it taste good and the machine that washes your cup). All of them depend primarily on the burning of the barrels and lumps of ancient biology now running short and threatening to wreck our climate.

5   We've somehow got to transform all that so that the ultimate power comes from somewhere else—and we have to do it without breaking the planet's economy. Money, in fact, becomes almost as important as units of energy in these calculations. If we can't do it at a reasonable cost, it's unlikely that we'll do it at all, both because we'll run out of cash and because we'll run out of politicians willing to vote for expensive projects.

REASONS FOR HOPE?

6   There are, happily, some real possibilities. To start with, we waste a lot of energy: The average American uses twice as much as the average Western European, even though our standard of living is no higher. The Belgians don't have a secret technology; they merely have a region that, because fuel prices have been high for 50 years, learned how to economize. Some of the difference is technological—building codes call for more insulation, and cars are held to higher mileage standards. But much of it is behavioral—people have learned to take the train instead of drive, to travel on the schedule of their community, not just their own whim.

7   Some of that will be hard to translate back onto our shores; our suburban sprawl is a machine for burning energy. But there's plenty we can do, beginning with replacing those incandescent light bulbs. Why not buy a hybrid car? Efficient appliances pay back in no time. If you take the commuter train, you can read a book on your way to work. In a strange way, the good news is that we're so energy obese that cutting the first, say, 20 percent won't be tough at all. It'll be like losing weight by cutting your hair.

8   After that, though, things get harder. Trade-offs start **emerging**. Some are huge: How much risk will you put up with from a nuclear power plant? Others are aesthetic: Community resistance to windmills on a nearby ridge or shoal seems to be **diminishing** as we begin to realize our actual energy needs. And some trade-offs are very personal: Would you be willing to eat a lot less meat? (By some measures, livestock production accounts for as much greenhouse gas as driving.) Or might you change your diet to eat close to home, forgoing those January strawberries from across the globe? Oh, and that overseas vacation? The jet to get you there will almost certainly burn more fuel than anything else you do all year.

9   The truth is, though, that none of these individual choices will add up fast enough to materially affect the amount of carbon in the

Emissions blow downwind from a coal-fired power plant in West Virginia, U.S.A.

atmosphere or the amount of oil left in the big fields of the Middle East. There simply aren't enough people paying real attention. The momentum of our economy is too strong, especially since we need change to come so quickly.

THE PRICE OF PROGRESS

10 We also need to fix the set of economic incentives that drives our energy system, so that capitalism can go to work helping us solve the problem. Until now, free markets have made the problem worse, not better. That's because they get no signal about carbon: Since there's no cost to pour it into the atmosphere, there's no way for markets to work their magic. But an international treaty that capped the amount of carbon we could emit would, in effect, put a price on CO_2, one high enough to reflect the damage it's doing.

11 This whole package of challenges adds up to the toughest thing humans have ever attempted. And part of the trouble is that we come at it with so much momentum: Energy use continues to shoot upward even as it becomes clear that we must **dramatically** change course. Delay of even a few years will be catastrophic. It's a timed test, where at some point in the not-too-distant future, we'll have to put our pencils down and simply live with the answers we've come up with. And since nature will grade us according to a rigid standard—our ability to survive—it will **require** every bit of **ingenuity**—technological, economic, and social—that we can muster.

---

apparatus: *n.* systems designed to perform a certain task

forgoing: *v.* doing without

momentum: *n.* the strength of a moving object

muster: *v.* to gather together, to assemble

A CARBON REDUCTION PLAN

Many sectors of the economy could save money by becoming more energy efficient. These savings could then be used to pay for improvements in how energy is generated. Combining these efforts could cut CO_2 emissions by over three billion tons a year in the U.S.A.

KEY SECTORS

POWER INDUSTRY
1,127 million tons/year

OTHER MEASURES
606

RENEWABLE ENERGY
521

BUILDINGS
729 million tons/year

OTHER
490

LIGHTING
239

INDUSTRY & WASTE
520 million tons/year

OTHER
247

REDUCING DIRECT EMISSIONS
273

FORESTRY & AGRICULTURE
486 million tons/year

OTHER
207

FOREST RECOVERY
279

TRANSPORTATION
357 million tons/year

OTHER
160

FUEL EFFICIENCY
197

CUTS IN CO_2 THAT SAVE MONEY

About 40 percent of possible cuts could come from measures that save billions of dollars a year (below). Most of these savings are found in building improvements, such as more efficient lighting and transportation improvements like better fuel efficiency.

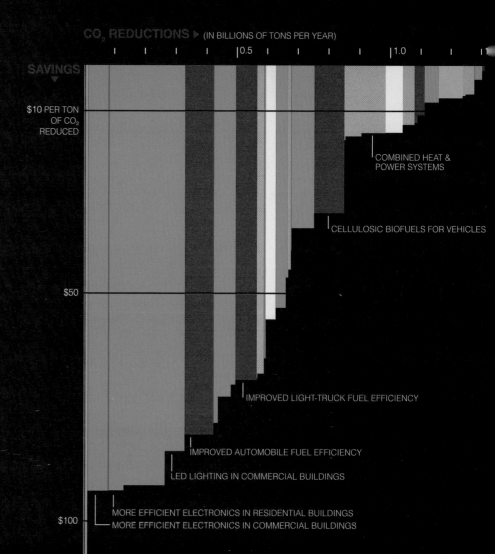

CO_2 REDUCTIONS ▷ (IN BILLIONS OF TONS PER YEAR)

0.5   1.0

SAVINGS ▼

$10 PER TON OF CO_2 REDUCED

COMBINED HEAT & POWER SYSTEMS

CELLULOSIC BIOFUELS FOR VEHICLES

$50

IMPROVED LIGHT-TRUCK FUEL EFFICIENCY

IMPROVED AUTOMOBILE FUEL EFFICIENCY

LED LIGHTING IN COMMERCIAL BUILDINGS

MORE EFFICIENT ELECTRONICS IN RESIDENTIAL BUILDINGS
MORE EFFICIENT ELECTRONICS IN COMMERCIAL BUILDINGS

$100

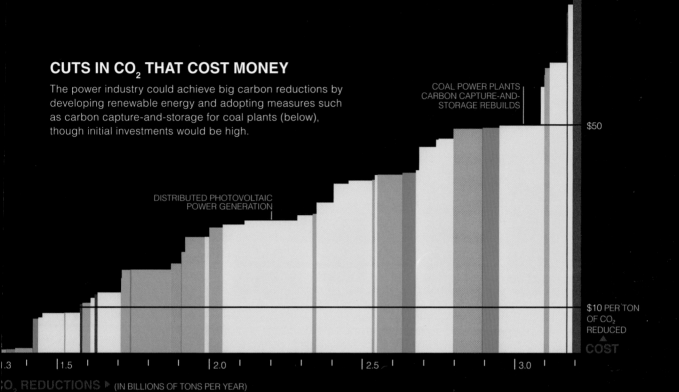

CUTS IN CO$_2$ THAT COST MONEY

The power industry could achieve big carbon reductions by developing renewable energy and adopting measures such as carbon capture-and-storage for coal plants (below), though initial investments would be high.

CAR HYBRIDIZATION ⎯

COAL POWER PLANTS
CARBON CAPTURE-AND-
STORAGE REBUILDS

$50

DISTRIBUTED PHOTOVOLTAIC
POWER GENERATION

$10 PER TON
OF CO$_2$
REDUCED
▲
COST

|.3 |1.5 | | | | |2.0 | | | |2.5 | | | |3.0 | |

CO$_2$ REDUCTIONS ▶ (IN BILLIONS OF TONS PER YEAR)

A worker installs a triple-glazed window in a new building in Washington, D.C., U.S.A. Investments like these can help reduce energy costs by up to 75 percent. But many firms hesitate to invest in efficiency if up-front costs seem too high or payback times too long.

GETTING THE MAIN IDEAS

A. **What is the overall message of the article?**

  a. Nuclear power has its risks but does significantly reduce CO_2 emissions.

  b. Difficult decisions need to be made about our energy production and use.

  c. Renewable energy is more practical than traditional forms of energy.

B. **How does McKibben develop his main message? Check (✔) the main idea of each of the following paragraphs.**

Paragraphs 1–2:

  _____ **a.** It will be hard to get away from fossil fuels because they have many benefits.

  _____ **b.** It shouldn't be hard to get away from fossil fuels. We're already using many renewables, such as solar.

Paragraphs 3–4:

  _____ **a.** Even though we are currently completely dependent on fossil fuels, it would be possible to switch to renewable sources in a few years.

  _____ **b.** There are some problems with renewable energy sources. In addition, we are currently almost completely dependent on fossil fuels.

Paragraph 5:

  _____ **a.** We need to change the way we finance power generation.

  _____ **b.** We have to change the way we get power, and we have to find an inexpensive way to do it.

Paragraphs 6–7:

  _____ **a.** There are plenty of things we can do right now to start saving energy, and some people are already doing them.

  _____ **b.** There are plenty of things we can do right now to start saving energy, but most people are unwilling to do these things.

Paragraph 8:

  _____ **a.** Changing the way we get energy may require some sacrifices.

  _____ **b.** Changing the way we get energy could have dangerous consequences.

Paragraph 10:

  _____ **a** We need to reduce our reliance on using free markets in order to motivate nations to reduce carbon emissions.

  _____ **b.** We need to find ways to financially reward nations that reduce carbon emissions.

UNDERSTANDING THE AUTHOR'S PURPOSE

In some academic texts, authors use comparisons to help support or set up their argument.

A. **McKibben compares fossil fuels and renewable energy. Use information from the passage to add any additional pros and cons to your chart on page 154.**

B. **Why does McKibben contrast these two forms of energy? Check (✔) the best reason.**

  _____ **a.** He's not happy that renewable energy is harder to produce than fossil fuels.

  _____ **b.** He wants to show that renewable forms of energy provide more jobs.

  _____ **c.** He's trying to show why it's difficult to switch to renewable forms.

UNDERSTANDING INFOGRAPHICS

A. **Use the information in the infographic on pages 158–159 to answer the questions below.**

1. Complete the statement about the purpose of the infographic.

   It shows that it is possible to reduce CO_2 by 3 billion tons a year in the U.S. through a

   combination of energy _____ and _____.

2. What do the colors in the graph represent?

   a. sectors of the economy   **b.** regions in the United States

3. What does the width of the bars represent?

   a. the amount of CO_2 that   **b.** the amount of money that
         can be reduced   must be spent

4. What does the length of the bars represent?

   a. an amount of CO_2 **b.** an amount of money

5. Which sector could save the most money by reducing CO_2?

   a. power industry   **b.** buildings   **c.** transportation

6. Give an example of what the transportation sector could do to save money and reduce CO_2 emissions.

   _____

7. Overall, which sector could reduce carbon emissions the most overall?

   a. power industry   **b.** buildings   **c.** transportation

8. The transportation sector could reduce CO_2 emissions by investing in car hybridization (cars that use more than one form of energy). How much investment would be needed for each ton of CO_2 reduced?

   _____

B. **Now complete a summary of the infographic.**

In the United States it is possible to _____ carbon emissions and _____
                                              1   2

money if certain industries such as building and transportation are made more energy

efficient. The money that is saved could then be used to _____ in renewable energy
                                                                3

sources, which are expensive.

BUILDING VOCABULARY

A. Complete the information with the words below.

alternatives	diminishing	emerging	intrinsic	require

Not only do fossil fuels contribute to climate change, their supplies are _____ .
₁

Environmental concerns, along with decreasing supplies of traditional energy, have

inspired us to look for other energy sources. Solar and wind power are two such sources

that have proven to be successful _____ to fossil fuels. There are some
₂

drawbacks to these technologies, though: Both _____ certain atmospheric
₃

conditions in order to function consistently. When there is no wind and the sky is cloudy,

for example, other energy sources need to be available.

It's clear that we need to continue to explore alternative energy sources. Several new

types of energy are currently under development. These _____ technologies
₄

include geothermal energy—energy from heat stored inside the Earth—and marine

energy—energy from the motion of the sea. All of these alternative energy sources have

two important _____ qualities that fossil fuels do not have. Because they are
₅

constantly replenished, they are renewable, and they produce few or no greenhouse

gases such as carbon dioxide (CO_2).

B. Match the sentence parts to complete the definitions.

1. If something is **concentrated**, ____.
2. If an event happens **dramatically**, ____.
3. If a thing is **equivalent** to another thing, ____.
4. **Ingenuity** is ____.
5. A **transition** is ____.

a. a change from one condition to another
b. it's equal in value or meaning
c. it's collected closely together
d. it makes a big impression
e. the quality of being inventive

C. Choose the word that best collocates with each of the words in bold.

1. **intrinsic** ____
   a. supply   b. value   c. source

2. **emerging** ____
   a. climates   b. emissions   c. markets

3. ____ **ingenuity**
   a. human   b. small   c. insignificant

4. ____ **transition**
   a. consistent   b. abrupt   c. changeable

GETTING MEANING FROM CONTEXT

A. **Find the following bold phrases in the passage. Choose the correct meaning.**

1. "All of them depend primarily on the burning of the barrels and lumps of ancient biology now **running short** and threatening to wreck our climate." (paragraph 4)

   a. being used up   **b.** getting closer

2. "And some **trade-offs** are very personal . . . " (paragraph 8)

   a. qualities that are not obvious   **b.** compromises

B. **Write answers to the following questions.**

1. What energy sources are we **running short** of?

   _____

2. What **trade-offs** would you be willing to accept in order to reduce CO_2 emissions?

   _____

   _____

CRITICAL THINKING

Inferring. Discuss the questions below with a partner.

1. Look again at paragraph 5 in the reading passage. How would you describe McKibben's tone? What words and phrases indicate this?

2. Look again at the final paragraph on page 157. What is McKibben's attitude about the challenges we face? What language does he use to convey this attitude?

EXPLORE MORE

Read the rest of McKibben's essay at nationalgeographic.com. According to McKibben, how has capitalism made the problem of CO_2 emissions worse? Share what you learn with the class.

Steam rises from a geothermal power station in Krafla, Iceland.

TEDTALKS

INNOVATING TO ZERO!

BILL GATES Philanthropist, TED speaker

🔊 "My full-time work," says Bill Gates, "is about the things that we need to invent and deliver to help the poorest 2 billion live better lives."

Tech visionary and Microsoft creator Bill Gates co-founded the Bill and Melinda Gates Foundation in order to improve the quality of life of people around the world. The foundation has donated large amounts of money to HIV/AIDS programs, libraries, agriculture research, and disaster relief. The foundation also works to provide funding for global health and education programs.

Bill and Melinda Gates base their activities on certain principles: They believe that it is important to take on big problems, such as extreme poverty; they are interested in solutions to problems, the kind that governments don't often support; and they believe that everyone in the world deserves to live a healthy, productive life.

---

visionary: *n.* a person with foresight, the ability to imagine the future

In this lesson, you are going to watch segments of Gates's 2010 TED Talk. Use the information above about Gates to answer each question.

1. What group of people is the Bill and Melinda Gates Foundation most trying to help?

   _____

2. What are three areas that the foundation supports?

   _____

   _____

3. What beliefs do Bill and Melinda Gates have about their work?

   _____

   _____

   _____

Gates's **idea worth spreading** is that in order for the world's people to thrive in the future—especially those who live in poverty—we need to invent technologies that will get CO_2 emissions down to zero with half the cost.

TARGET ZERO

PREDICTING

A. Look at the graph showing falling energy prices. What do you think might be the benefits of this trend? Discuss with a partner.

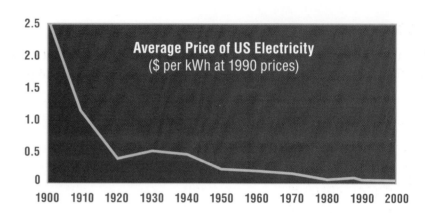

Average Price of US Electricity ($ per kWh at 1990 prices)

B. Watch (▶) the first part of Gates's talk. Then use the information (a–g) to complete the flow chart showing the problems with low-cost energy.

a. Causes crop failure

b. Causes more CO_2 to be released into the atmosphere

c. Contributes to climate change

d. Increases severity of droughts and floods

e. Leads to higher use of energy

f. Leads to starvation, uncertainty, and unrest

g. Low cost of energy

g	→	c	→	b	→	c	→	d	→	a	→	f
1		2		3		4		5		6		7

UNDERSTANDING MAIN IDEAS

Write short answers to the questions about this part of Gates's talk.

1. What happens when CO_2 emissions enter the atmosphere?

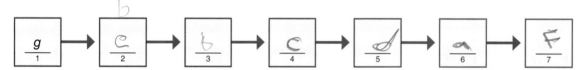

increse temperature then in heather equal systems collapses

2. Is it enough to cut CO_2 emissions by half? Why or why not?

No, because the temperature continues to rise

CRITICAL THINKING

Analyzing. Discuss these questions with a partner.

1. What will be the effects of cutting CO_2 emissions down to zero?

2. Do you think it's possible to get CO_2 emissions down to zero? Why or why not?

THE NEED FOR A MIRACLE

PREDICTING

In the next segment of his talk, Gates presents a formula for calculating CO_2 emissions. What do you think the four factors (P, S, E, C) are? Discuss with a partner.

CO_2 = P _People_ × S _Services per person_ × E _Energy per person_ × C _CO_2_

UNDERSTANDING MAIN IDEAS

Now watch (▶) this segment of the TED Talk and check your answers to the Predicting activity. Choose the correct summary of this part of Gates's talk.

a. We need to reduce at least one of these factors to zero in order to deal with global warming.

b. We need to urgently reduce all four factors in order to bring CO_2 emissions to zero.

UNDERSTANDING KEY DETAILS

Complete the chart below using the ideas (a–f) that Gates presents.

a. Better health care

b. Innovations in lighting, types of cars, different ways of building

c. Air transportation changes will have limited impact

d. Most forms of energy used today produce CO_2

e. Getting rid of poverty requires more food, heating, etc.

f. The richest one billion people can make some reductions

	P	S	E	C
Ways to reduce or limit growth	a	f e	b	create an "energy miracle"
Problems with reducing or limiting growth		e	c	

CRITICAL THINKING

Interpreting. What does Gates mean when he says it will take "a miracle" to reduce CO_2?

TEDTALKS

PART 3

A WISH FOR THE PLANET

UNDERSTANDING KEY DETAILS

What does Gates say we need to achieve by 2020 and 2050? Watch (▶) the next segment of his talk and complete the report cards. Two items are extra.

a. 10   **b.** 20   **c.** 80   **d.** deploy   **e.** make progress in   **f.** start

2020 Report Card		2050 Report Card	
reduce CO_2 emissions by _2020_ 2 percent	☐	reduce CO_2 emissions by _80_% percent	☐
_c_ developing zero-emission innovations	☐	_d_ zero-emission innovations in developed countries	☑

SUMMARIZING INFORMATION

A. Read the following excerpt from this part of the talk. What is Gates's wish? Discuss with a partner.

> ❝ So this is a wish. It's a very concrete wish that we invent this technology. If you gave me only one wish for the next 50 years—I could pick who's president, I could pick a vaccine, which is something I love, or I could pick that this thing that's half the cost with no CO_2 gets invented—this is the wish I would pick. This is the one with the greatest impact. If we don't get this wish, the division between the people who think short term and long term will be terrible, between the U.S. and China, between poor countries and rich, and most of all the lives of those 2 billion will be far worse. ❞

B. Choose the statement that best summarizes Gates's main idea in the last part of his talk.

a. Hoping for a market-based solution to the crisis is not enough; we need strong action now by leading governments.

b. Researchers have spent too long looking for new solutions; we need to agree on the best option and stick with it.

c. We need more research funding, more market incentives, and a more rational dialogue in order to achieve our goal.

EXPLORE MORE

Watch Bill Gates's full TED Talk at TED.com. How does Gates think the TerraPower innovation will help get CO_2 levels to zero? Share what you find out with a partner.

Project

A man rides his bike down an alley in San Francisco, U.S.A. San Francisco has seen bike ridership increase by close to 100% in the last decade.

A. **Think of a trade-off that you can make in order to save energy. Think of an activity that you can realistically do for one week. Choose one of the following, or think of your own ideas.**

- Stop eating meat.
- Read instead of watching TV.
- Walk instead of driving or taking the bus.
- Wash in cold water instead of hot water.
- Don't buy anything new.

1. Commit to doing your trade-off for one week. Keep a journal during the week. Use it to record information such as:

   - What is your trade-off? What are you actually doing each day?
   - How does it make you feel?
   - How is it affecting your life?
   - How is it saving energy or improving the environment?
   - What other benefits does it have?
   - Can you continue doing this after the one-week period? Why or why not?

2. Use your journal to create a two-minute presentation on your one-week trade-off experience.

B. **Work in small groups.**

- Give your presentations.
- As you listen, take notes.
- At the end, review your notes.
- Have a class discussion. Which trade-off do you think saves the most energy? Which trade-off seems like the greatest sacrifice?
- Which might be the easiest or hardest to maintain for more than a week? What are some other trade-offs you might try?

EXPLORE MORE

Learn more about energy solutions by exploring the TED Talks on the playlist "The end of oil?" at TED.com. Share what you learn with the class.

TEDTALK VIDEO TRANSCRIPTS

Unit 1

BRIAN COX

Why We Need the Explorers

Part 1

We live in difficult and challenging economic times, of course. And one of the first victims of difficult economic times, I think, is public spending of any kind, but certainly in the firing line at the moment is public spending for science, and particularly curiosity-led science and exploration. So I want to try and convince you in about 15 minutes that that's a ridiculous and ludicrous thing to do.

[. . .] The first thing I want to say, and this is straight from *Wonders of the Solar System,* is that our exploration of the solar system and the universe has shown us that it is indescribably beautiful. This is a picture that actually was sent back by the Cassini space probe around Saturn, after we'd finished filming *Wonders of the Solar System.* So it isn't in the series. It's of the moon Enceladus. So that big sweeping, white sphere in the corner is Saturn, which is actually in the background of the picture. And that crescent there is the moon Enceladus, which is about as big as the British Isles. It's about 500 kilometers in diameter. So, tiny moon. What's fascinating and beautiful . . . this an unprocessed picture, by the way, I should say, it's black and white, straight from Saturnian orbit.

What's beautiful is, you can probably see on the limb there some faint, sort of, wisps of almost smoke rising up from the limb. This is how we visualize that in *Wonders of the Solar System.* It's a beautiful graphic. What we found out were that those faint wisps are actually fountains of ice rising up from the surface of this tiny moon. That's fascinating and beautiful in itself, but we think that the mechanism for powering those fountains requires there to be lakes of liquid water beneath the surface of this moon. And what's important about that is that, on our planet, on Earth, wherever we find liquid water, we find life. So, to find strong evidence of liquid, pools of liquid, beneath the surface of a moon 750 million miles away from the Earth is really quite astounding. So what we're saying, essentially, is maybe that's a habitat for life in the solar system. Well, let me just say, that was a graphic. I just want to show this picture. That's one more picture of Enceladus. This is when Cassini flew beneath Enceladus. So it made a very low pass, just a few hundred kilometers above the surface. And so this, again, a real picture of the ice fountains rising up into space, absolutely beautiful.

[. . .] Our exploration of the solar system has taught us that the solar system is beautiful. It may also have pointed the way to answering one of the most profound questions that you can possibly ask, which is: "Are we alone in the universe?" Is there any other use to exploration and science, other than just a sense of wonder? Well, there is. This is a very famous picture taken, actually, on my first Christmas Eve, December 24th, 1968, when I was about eight months old. It was taken by Apollo 8 as it went around the back of the moon. Earthrise from Apollo 8. A famous picture; many people have said that it's the picture that saved 1968, which was a turbulent year—the student riots in Paris, the height of the Vietnam War. The reason many people think that about this picture, and Al Gore has said it many times, actually, on the stage at TED, is that this picture, arguably, was the beginning of the environmental movement. Because, for the first time, we saw our world, not as a solid, immovable, kind of indestructible place, but as a very small, fragile-looking world just hanging against the blackness of space.

Part 2

What's also not often said about the space exploration, about the Apollo program, is the economic contribution it made. I mean, while you can make arguments that it was wonderful and a tremendous achievement and delivered pictures like this, it cost a lot, didn't it? Well, actually, many studies have been done about the economic effectiveness, the economic impact of Apollo. The biggest one was in 1975 by Chase Econometrics. And it showed that for every $1 spent on Apollo, 14 came back into the U.S. economy. So the Apollo program paid for itself in inspiration, in engineering, achievement and, I think, in inspiring young scientists and engineers 14 times over. So exploration can pay for itself.

What about scientific discovery? What about driving innovation? Well, this looks like a picture of virtually nothing. What it is, is a picture of the spectrum of hydrogen. See, back in the 1880s, 1890s, many scientists, many observers, looked at the light given off from atoms. And they saw strange pictures like this. What you're seeing when you put it through a prism is that you heat hydrogen up and it doesn't just glow like a white light, it just emits light at particular colors, a red one, a light blue one, some dark blue ones. Now that led to an understanding of atomic structure because the way that's explained is atoms are a single nucleus with electrons going around them. And the electrons can only be in particular places. And when they jump up to the next place they can be, and fall back down again, they emit light at particular colors.

And so the fact that atoms, when you heat them up, only emit light at very specific colors, was one of the key drivers that led to the development of the quantum theory, the theory of the structure of atoms.

[. . .] Now, that sounds esoteric, and indeed it was an esoteric pursuit, but the quantum theory quickly led to an understanding of the behaviors of electrons in materials like silicon, for example. The way that silicon behaves, the fact that you can build transistors, is a purely quantum phenomenon. So without that curiosity-driven understanding of the structure of atoms, which led to this rather esoteric theory, quantum mechanics, then we wouldn't have transistors, we wouldn't have silicon chips, we wouldn't have pretty much the basis of our modern economy.

[. . .] This is a beautiful quote that I found—we're talking about serendipity there—from Alexander Fleming: "When I woke up just after dawn on September 28, 1928, I certainly didn't plan to revolutionize all medicine by discovering the world's first antibiotic." Now, the explorers of the world of the atom did not intend to invent the transistor. And they certainly didn't intend to describe the mechanics of supernova explosions, which eventually told us where the building blocks of life were synthesized in the universe. So, I think science can be— serendipity is important. It can be beautiful. It can reveal quite astonishing things. It can also, I think, finally reveal the most profound ideas to us about our place in the universe and really the value of our home planet.

[. . .] The argument has always been made, and it will always be made, that we know enough about the universe. You could have made it in the 1920s; you wouldn't have had penicillin. You could have made it in the 1890s; you wouldn't have the transistor. And it's made today in these difficult economic times: *Surely, we know enough. We don't need to discover anything else about our universe.*

Let me leave the last words to someone who's rapidly becoming a hero of mine, Humphrey Davy, who did his science at the turn of the 19th century. He was clearly under assault all the time. "We know enough at the turn of the 19th century. Just exploit it; just build things." He said this, he said, "Nothing is more fatal to the progress of the human mind than to presume that our views of science are ultimate, that our triumphs are complete, that there are no mysteries in nature, and that there are no new worlds to conquer."

This is an edited version of Cox's 2010 TED Talk. To watch the full talk, visit TED.com.

DIANA LAUFENBERG

How to Learn? From Mistakes

Part 1

I have been teaching for a long time, and in doing so have acquired a body of knowledge about kids and learning that I really wish more people would understand about the potential of students. In 1931, my grandmother—bottom left for you guys over here—graduated from the eighth grade. She went to school to get the information because that's where the information lived. It was in the books; it was inside the teacher's head; and she needed to go there to get the information, because that's how you learned. Fast-forward a generation: This is the one-room schoolhouse, Oak Grove, where my father went to a one-room schoolhouse. And he again had to travel to the school to get the information from the teacher, stored it in the only portable memory he has, which is inside his own head, and take it with him, because that is how information was being transported from teacher to student and then used in the world. When I was a kid, we had a set of encyclopedias at my house. It was purchased the year I was born, and it was extraordinary, because I did not have to wait to go to the library to get to the information. The information was inside my house, and it was awesome. This was different than either generation had experienced before, and it changed the way I interacted with information even at just a small level. But the information was closer to me. I could get access to it.

[. . .] Fast-forward to Pennsylvania, where I find myself today. I teach at the Science Leadership Academy, which is a partnership school between the Franklin Institute and the school district of Philadelphia. We are a 9 through 12 public school, but we do school quite differently. I moved there primarily to be part of a learning environment that validated the way that I knew that kids learned, and that really wanted to investigate what was possible when you are willing to let go of some of the paradigms of the past, of information scarcity when my grandmother was in school and when my father was in school and even when I was in school, and to a moment when we have information surplus. So what do you do when the information is all around you? Why do you have kids come to school if they no longer have to come there to get the information?

Part 2

In Philadelphia we have a one-to-one laptop program, so the kids are bringing in laptops with them every day, taking them home, getting access to information. And here's the thing that you need to get comfortable with when you've given the tool to acquire information to students, is that you have to be comfortable with this idea of allowing kids to fail as part of the learning process. We deal right now in the educational landscape with an infatuation with the culture of one right answer that can be properly bubbled on the average multiple-choice test, and I am here to share with you: It is not learning. That is the absolute wrong thing to ask, to tell kids to never be wrong. To ask them to always have the right answer doesn't allow them to learn. So we did this project, and this is one of the artifacts of the project. I almost never show them off because of the issue of the idea of failure.

My students produced these infographics as a result of a unit that we decided to do at the end of the year responding to the oil spill. I asked them to take the examples that we were seeing of the infographics that existed in a lot of mass media, and take a look at what were the interesting components of it, and produce one for themselves of a different man-made disaster from American history. And they had certain criteria to do it. They were a little uncomfortable with it, because we'd never done this before, and they didn't know exactly how to do it. They can talk—they're very smooth, and they can write very, very well, but asking them to communicate ideas in a different way was a little uncomfortable for them. But I gave them the room to just do the thing. Go create. Go figure it out. Let's see what we can do. And the student that persistently turns out the best visual product did not disappoint. This was done in like two or three days. And this is the work of the student that consistently did it.

And when I sat the students down, I said, "Who's got the best one?" And they immediately went, "There it is." Didn't read anything. "There it is." And I said, "Well, what makes it great?" And they're like, "Oh, the design's good, and he's using good color. And there's some . . ." And they went through all that we processed out loud. And I said, "Go read it." And they're like,

"Oh, that one wasn't so awesome." And then we went to another one—it didn't have great visuals, but it had great information—and spent an hour talking about the learning process, because it wasn't about whether or not it was perfect, or whether or not it was what I could create. It asked them to create for themselves, and it allowed them to fail, process, learn from. And when we do another round of this in my class this year, they will do better this time, because learning has to include an amount of failure, because failure is instructional in the process.

[. . .] The main point is that if we continue to look at education as if it's about coming to school to get the information and not about experiential learning, empowering student voice, and embracing failure, we're missing the mark. And everything that everybody is talking about today isn't possible if we keep having an educational system that does not value these qualities, because we won't get there with a standardized test, and we won't get there with a culture of one right answer. We know how to do this better, and it's time to do better.

This is an edited version of Laufenberg's 2010 TED Talk. To watch the full talk, visit TED.com.

SHERYL SANDBERG
Why We Have Too Few Women Leaders

Part 1

So for any of us in this room today, let's start out by admitting we're lucky. We don't live in the world our mothers lived in, our grandmothers lived in, where career choices for women were so limited. And if you're in this room today, most of us grew up in a world where we had basic civil rights, and amazingly, we still live in a world where some women don't have them. But all that aside, we still have a problem, and it's a real problem. And the problem is this: Women are not making it to the top of any profession anywhere in the world. The numbers tell the story quite clearly. 190 heads of state—nine are women. Of all the people in parliament in the world, 13 percent are women. In the corporate sector, women at the top, C-level jobs, board seats—tops out at 15, 16 percent. The numbers have not moved since 2002 and are going in the wrong direction. And even in the non-profit world, a world we sometimes think of as being led by more women, women at the top: 20 percent.

We also have another problem, which is that women face harder choices between professional success and personal fulfillment. A recent study in the U.S. showed that, of married senior managers, two-thirds of the married men had children and only one-third of the married women had children.

[. . .] So the question is, how are we going to fix this? How do we change these numbers at the top? How do we make this different? I want to start out by saying, I talk about this—about keeping women in the workforce—because I really think that's the answer. In the high-income part of our workforce, in the people who end up at the top—Fortune 500 CEO jobs, or the equivalent in other industries—the problem, I am convinced, is that women are dropping out. Now people talk about this a lot, and they talk about things like flextime and mentoring and programs companies should have to train women. I want to talk about none of that today, even though that's all really important. Today, I want to focus on what we can do as individuals. What are the messages we need to tell ourselves? What are the messages we tell the women who work with and for us? What are the messages we tell our daughters?

Now, at the outset, I want to be very clear that this speech comes with no judgments. I don't have the right answer. I don't even have it for myself. I left San Francisco, where I live, on Monday, and I was getting on the plane for this conference. And my daughter, who's three, when I dropped her off at preschool, did that whole hugging-the-leg, crying, "Mommy, don't get on the plane" thing. This is hard. I feel guilty sometimes. I know no women, whether they're at home or whether they're in the workforce, who don't feel that sometimes. So I'm not saying that staying in the workforce is the right thing for everyone.

My talk today is about what the messages are if you do want to stay in the workforce, and I think there are three. One, sit at the table. Two, make your partner a real partner. And three, don't leave before you leave.

[. . .]

Part 2

[W]omen systematically underestimate their own abilities. If you test men and women, and you ask them questions on totally objective criteria like GPAs, men get it wrong slightly high, and women get it wrong slightly low. Women do not negotiate for themselves in the workforce. A study in the last two years of people entering the workforce out of college showed that 57 percent of boys entering, or men, I guess, are negotiating their first salary, and only seven percent of women. And most importantly, men attribute their success to themselves, and women attribute it to other external factors. If you ask men why they did a good job, they'll say, "I'm awesome. Obviously. Why are you even asking?" If you ask women why they did a good job, what they'll say is someone helped them, they got lucky, they worked really hard. Why does this matter? Boy, it matters a lot because no one gets to the corner office by sitting on the side, not at the table, and no one gets the promotion if they don't think they deserve their success, or they don't even understand their own success.

I wish the answer were easy. I wish I could just go tell all the young women I work for, all these fabulous women, "Believe in yourself and negotiate for yourself. Own your own success." I wish I could tell that to my daughter. But it's not that simple. Because what the data shows, above all else, is one thing, which is that success and likeability are positively correlated for men and negatively correlated for women. And everyone's nodding, because we all know this to be true.

There's a really good study that shows this really well. There's a famous Harvard Business School study on a woman named Heidi Roizen. And she's an operator in a company in Silicon Valley, and she uses her contacts to become a very successful venture capitalist. In 2002—not so long ago—a professor who was then at Columbia University took that case and made it [Howard] Roizen. And he gave the case out, both of them, to two groups of students. He changed exactly one word: *Heidi* to *Howard*. But that one word made a really big difference. He then surveyed the students, and the good news was the students, both men and women, thought Heidi and Howard were equally competent, and that's good. The bad news was that everyone liked Howard. He's a great guy. You want to work for him. You want to spend the day fishing with him. But Heidi? Not so sure. She's a little out for herself. She's a little political. You're not sure you'd want to work for her. This is the complication. We have to tell our daughters and our colleagues, we have to tell ourselves to believe we got the A, to reach for the promotion, to sit at the table, and we have to do it in a world where, for them, there are sacrifices they will make for that, even though for their brothers, there are not.

The saddest thing about all of this is that it's really hard to remember this. And I'm about to tell a story which is truly embarrassing for me, but I think important. I gave this talk at Facebook not so long ago to about 100 employees, and a couple hours later, there was a young woman who works there sitting outside my little desk, and she wanted to talk to me. I said, OK, and she sat down, and we talked. And she said, "I learned something today. I learned that I need to keep my hand up." I said, "What do you mean?" She said, "Well, you're giving this talk, and you said you were going to take two more questions. And I had my hand up with lots of other people, and you took two more questions. And I put my hand down, and I noticed all the women put their hand down, and then you took more questions, only from the men." And I thought to myself, wow, if it's me—who cares about this, obviously—giving this talk—and during this talk, I can't even notice that the men's hands are still raised, and the women's hands are still raised, how good are we as managers of our companies and our organizations at seeing that the men are reaching for opportunities more than women? We've got to get women to sit at the table.

[. . .] My generation really, sadly, is not going to change the numbers at the top. They're just not moving. We are not going to get to where 50 percent of the population—in my generation, there will not be 50 percent of [women] at the top of any industry. But I'm hopeful that future generations can. I think a world that was run where half of our countries and half of our companies were run by women, would be a better world. And it's not just because people would know where the women's bathrooms are, even though that would be very helpful. I think it would be a better world. I have two children. I have a five-year-old son and a two-year-old daughter. I want my son to have a choice to contribute fully in the workforce or at home, and I want my daughter to have the choice to not just succeed, but to be liked for her accomplishments.

This is an edited version of Sandberg's 2010 TED Talk. To watch the full talk, visit TED.com.

Unit 4

J.J. ABRAMS
The Mystery Box

Part 1

[. . .] Why do I do so much stuff that involves mystery? And I started trying to figure it out. And I started thinking about why do I do any of what I do, and I started thinking about my grandfather. I loved my grandfather. Harry Kelvin was his name, my mother's father. He died in 1986. He was an amazing guy. And one of the reasons he was amazing: After World War II, he began an electronics company. He started selling surplus parts, kits, to schools and stuff. So he had this incredible curiosity. As a kid, I saw him come over to me with radios and telephones and all sorts of things. And he'd open them up, he'd unscrew them, and reveal the inner workings—which many of us, I'm sure, take for granted. But it's an amazing gift to give a kid. To open up this thing and show how it works and why it works and what it is. He was the ultimate deconstructor, in many ways.

[. . .] He sort of humored my obsession to other things, too, like magic. The thing is, we'd go to this magic store in New York City called Lou Tannen's Magic. It was this great magic store. It was a crappy little building in Midtown, but you'd be in the elevator, the elevator would open—there'd be this little, small magic store. You'd be in the magic store. And it was just, it was a magical place. So I got all these sort of magic tricks. Oh, here. I'll show you. This is the kind of thing. So it would be like, you know. Right? Which is good, but now I can't move. Now, I have to do this, the rest of the thing, like this. I'm like, "Oh, wow. Look at my computer over there!"

Anyway, so one of the things that I bought at the magic store was this: Tannen's Mystery Magic Box. The premise behind the mystery magic box was the following: 15 dollars buys you 50 dollars worth of magic. Which is a savings. Now, I bought this decades ago and I'm not kidding. If you look at this, you'll see it's never been opened. But I've had this forever. Now, I was looking at this, it was in my office, as it always is, on the shelf, and I was thinking, why have I not opened this? And why have I kept it? Because I'm not a pack rat. I don't keep everything, but for some reason I haven't opened this box. And I felt like there was a key to this, somehow, in talking about something at TED that I haven't discussed before, and bored people elsewhere. So I thought, maybe there's something with this. I started thinking about it. And there was this giant question mark. I love the design, for what it's worth, of this thing. And I started thinking, why haven't I opened it?

And I realized that I haven't opened it because it represents something important—to me. It represents my grandfather. Am I allowed to cry at TED? Because—no, I'm not going to cry. But—the thing is, that it represents infinite possibility. It represents hope. It represents potential. And what I love about this box, and what I realize I sort of do in whatever it is that I do, is I find myself drawn to infinite possibility, that sense of potential. And I realize that mystery is the catalyst for imagination. Now, it's not the most groundbreaking idea, but when I started to think that maybe there are times when mystery is more important than knowledge, I started getting interested in this.

[. . .] What's a bigger mystery box than a movie theater? You know? You go to the theater, you're just so excited to see anything. The moment the lights go down is often the best part, you know? And you're full of that amazing—that feeling of excited anticipation. And often, the movie's, like, there and it's going, and then something happens and you go, "Oh—" and then something else, and you're, "Mmm . . ." Now, when it's a great movie, you're along for the ride 'cause you're willing to give yourself to it.

Part 2

[. . .] This is something online; I don't know if you've seen it before. Six years ago, they did this. This is an online thing done by guys who had some visual effects experience. But the point was that they were doing things that were using these mystery boxes that they had—everyone has now. What I've realized is what my grandfather did for me when I was a kid, everyone has access to now. You don't need to have my grandfather, though you wished you had. But I have to tell you—this is a guy doing stuff on a Quadra 950 computer—the resolution's a little bit low—using Infinity software they stopped making 15 years ago. He's doing stuff that looks as amazing as stuff I've seen released from Hollywood.

The most incredible sort of mystery, I think, is now the question of what comes next. Because it is now democratized. So now, the creation of media is—it's everywhere. The stuff that I was lucky and begging for to get when I was a kid is now ubiquitous. And so, there's an amazing sense of opportunity out there. And when I think of the filmmakers who exist out there now who would have been silenced, you know—who have been silenced in the past—it's a very exciting thing.

I used to say in classes and lectures and stuff, to someone who wants to write, "Go! Write! Do your thing." It's free, you know, you don't need permission to go write. But now I can say, "Go make your movie!" There's nothing stopping you from going out there and getting the technology. You can lease, rent, buy stuff off the shelf that is either as good, or just as good, as the stuff that's being used by the, you know, quote unquote "legit people." No community is best served when only the elite have control. And I feel like this is an amazing opportunity to see what else is out there.

Part 3

When I did *Mission: Impossible III*, we had amazing visual effects stuff. ILM did the effects; it was incredible. And sort of like my dream to be involved. And there are a couple of sequences in the movie, like these couple of moments I'll show you. There's that.

OK, obviously I have an obsession with big crazy explosions. So my favorite visual effect in the movie is the one I'm about to show you. And it's a scene in which Tom's character wakes up. He's drowsy. He's crazy—out of it. And the guy wakes up, and he shoves this gun in his nose and shoots this little capsule into his brain that he's going to use later to kill him, as bad guys do.

Bad Guy: Good morning.

OK, now. When we shot that scene, we were there doing it, the actor who had the gun, an English actor, Eddie Marsan—sweetheart, great guy—he kept taking the gun and putting it into Tom's nose, and it was hurting Tom's nose. And I learned this very early on in my career: Don't hurt Tom's nose. There are three things you don't want to do. Number two is: Don't hurt Tom's nose. So Eddie has this gun—and he's the greatest guy—he's this really sweet English guy. He's like, "Sorry, I don't want to hurt you." I'm like—you gotta—we have to make this look good. And I realized that we had to do something 'cause it wasn't working just as it was. And I literally, like, thought back to what I would have done using the Super 8 camera that my grandfather got me sitting in that room, and I realized that hand didn't have to be Eddie Marsan's. It could be Tom's. And Tom would know just how hard to push the gun. He wouldn't hurt himself.

So we took his hand and we painted it to look a little bit more like Eddie's. We put it in Eddie's sleeve, and so the hand that you see—I'll show you again, that's not Eddie's hand, that's Tom's. So Tom is playing two roles. And he didn't ask for any more money. So here, here. Watch it again. There he is. He's waking up. He's drowsy, been through a lot. Tom's hand. Tom's hand. Tom's hand. Anyway. So. Thanks. So you don't need the greatest technology to do things that can work in movies. And the mystery box, in honor of my grandfather, stays closed. Thank you.

This is an edited version of Abrams' 2007 TED Talk. To watch the full talk, visit TED.com.

BONO

The Good News on Poverty
(Yes, There's Good News)

Part 1

[. . .] So I thought, forget the rock opera, forget the bombast, my usual tricks. The only thing singing today would be the facts, for I have truly embraced my inner nerd.

So exit the rock star. Enter the evidence-based activist, the factivist. →activist who uses facts.

Because what the facts are telling us is that the long, slow journey, humanity's long, slow journey of equality, is actually speeding up. Look at what's been achieved. Look at the pictures these data sets print. Since the year 2000, since the turn of the millennium, there are eight million more AIDS patients getting life-saving antiretroviral drugs. Malaria: There are eight countries in sub-Saharan Africa that have their death rates cut by 75 percent. For kids under five, child mortality, kids under five, it's down by 2.65 million a year. That's a rate of 7,256 children's lives saved each day. Wow. Wow.

Let's just stop for a second, actually, and think about that. Have you read anything anywhere in the last week that is remotely as important as that number? Wow. Great news. It drives me nuts that most people don't seem to know this news. Seven thousand kids a day. Here's two of them. This is Michael and Benedicta, and they're alive thanks in large part to Dr. Patricia Asamoah—she's amazing—and the Global Fund, which all of you financially support, whether you know it or not. And the Global Fund provides antiretroviral drugs that stop mothers from passing HIV to their kids. This fantastic news didn't happen by itself. It was fought for, it was campaigned for, it was innovated for. And this great news gives birth to even more great news, because the historic trend is this. The number of people living in back-breaking, soul-crushing extreme poverty has declined from 43 percent of the world's population in 1990 to 33 percent by 2000 and then to 21 percent by 2010. Give it up for that. Halved. Halved.

Now, the rate is still too high—still too many people unnecessarily losing their lives. There's still work to do. But it's heart-stopping. It's mind-blowing stuff. And if you live on less than $1.25 a day, if you live in that kind of poverty, this is not just data. This is everything. If you're a parent who wants the best for your kids—and I am—this rapid transition is a route out of despair and into hope. And guess what! If the trajectory continues, look where the amount of people living on $1.25 a day gets to by 2030. Can't be true, can it? That's what the data is telling us. If the trajectory continues, we get to, wow, the zero zone.

[. . .]

Part 2

So why aren't we jumping up and down about this? Well, the opportunity is real, but so is the jeopardy. We can't get this done until we really accept that we can get this done. Look at this graph. It's called inertia. It's how we screw it up. And the next one is really beautiful. It's called momentum. And it's how we can bend the arc of history down towards zero, just doing the things that we know work.

So inertia versus momentum. There is jeopardy, and of course, the closer you get, it gets harder. We know the obstacles that are in our way right now, in difficult times. In fact, today in your capital, in difficult times, some who mind the nation's purse want to cut life-saving programs like the Global Fund. But you can do something about that. You can tell politicians that these cuts [can cost] lives.

Right now today, in Oslo as it happens, oil companies are fighting to keep secret their payments to governments for extracting oil in developing countries. You can do something about that, too. You can join the ONE Campaign, and leaders like Mo Ibrahim, the telecom entrepreneur. We're pushing for laws that make sure that at least some of the wealth under the ground ends up in the hands of the people living above it.

And right now, we know that the biggest disease of all is not a disease. It's corruption. But there's a vaccine for that, too. It's called transparency, open data sets, something the TED community is really on it. Daylight, you could call it, transparency. And technology is really turbocharging this. It's getting harder to hide if you're doing bad stuff.

So let me tell you about the U-report, which I'm really excited about. It's 150,000 millennials all across Uganda, young people armed with 2G phones, an SMS social network exposing government corruption and demanding to know what's in the budget and how their money is being spent. This is exciting stuff.

Look, once you have these tools, you can't not use them. Once you have this knowledge, you can't un-know it. You can't delete this data from your brain, but you can delete the cliched image of supplicant, impoverished peoples not taking control of their own lives. You can erase that, you really can, because it's not true anymore.

It's transformational. 2030? By 2030, robots, not just serving us Guinness, but drinking it. By the time we get there, every place with a rough semblance of governance might actually be on their way.

So I'm here to—I guess we're here to try and infect you with this virtuous, data-based virus, the one we call <u>factivism.</u> It's

not going to kill you. In fact, it could save countless lives. I guess we in the ONE Campaign would love you to be contagious, spread it, share it, pass it on. By doing so, you will join us and countless others in what I truly believe is the greatest adventure ever taken, the ever-demanding journey of equality.

[. . .]

This is an edited version of Bono's 2013 TED Talk. To watch the full talk, visit TED.com.

Unit 6

BEN KACYRA

Ancient Wonders Captured in 3-D

Part 1

I'd like to start with a short story. It's about a little boy whose father was a history buff and who used to take him by the hand to visit the ruins of an ancient metropolis on the outskirts of their camp. They would always stop by to visit these huge winged bulls that used to guard the gates of that ancient metropolis, and the boy used to be scared of these winged bulls, but at the same time they excited him. And the dad used to use those bulls to tell the boy stories about that civilization and their work.

Let's fast-forward to the San Francisco Bay Area many decades later, where I started a technology company that brought the world its first 3D laser scanning system. Let me show you how it works.

[Video] *Female Voice: Long-range laser scanning works by sending out a pulse that's a laser beam of light. The system measures the beam's time of flight, recording the time it takes for the light to hit a surface and make its return. With two mirrors, the scanner calculates the beam's horizontal and vertical angles, giving accurate x, y, and z coordinates. The point is then recorded into a 3D visualization program. All of this happens in seconds.*

You can see here, these systems are extremely fast. They collect millions of points at a time with very high accuracy and very high resolution. A surveyor with traditional survey tools would be hard-pressed to produce maybe 500 points in

a whole day. These babies would be producing something like ten thousand points a second. So, as you can imagine, this was a paradigm shift in the survey and construction as well as in reality-capture industry.

Approximately ten years ago, my wife and I started a foundation to do good, and right about that time, the magnificent Bamiyan Buddhas, hundred and eighty foot tall in Afghanistan, were blown up by the Taliban. They were gone in an instant. And unfortunately, there was no detailed documentation of these Buddhas. This clearly devastated me, and I couldn't help but wonder about the fate of my old friends, the winged bulls, and the fate of the many, many heritage sites all over the world. Both my wife and I were so touched by this that we decided to expand the mission of our foundation to include digital heritage preservation of world sites. We called the project CyArk, which stands for Cyber Archive.

Part 2

To date, with the help of a global network of partners, we've completed close to fifty projects. Let me show you some of them: Chichen Itza, Rapa Nui—and what you're seeing here are the cloud of points—Babylon, Rosslyn Chapel, Pompeii, and our latest project, Mt. Rushmore, which happened to be one of our most challenging projects. As you see here, we had to develop a special rig to bring the scanner up close and personal. The results of our work in the field are used to produce media and deliverables to be used by conservators and researchers. We also produce media for dissemination to the public—free through the CyArk website. These would be used for education, cultural tourism, etc.

What you're looking at in here is a 3D viewer that we developed that would allow the display and manipulation of [the] cloud of points in real time, cutting sections through them and extracting dimensions. This happens to be the cloud of points for Tikal. In here you see a traditional 2D architectural engineering drawing that's used for preservation, and of course we tell the stories through fly-throughs. And here, this is a fly-through the cloud of points of Tikal, and here you see it rendered and photo-textured with the photography that we take of the site. And so this is not a video. This is actual 3D points with two- to three-millimeter accuracy. And of course the data can be used to develop 3D models that are very accurate and very detailed. And here you're looking at a model that's extracted from the cloud of points for Stirling Castle. It's used for studies, for visualization, as well as for education.

And finally, we produce mobile apps that include narrated virtual tools. The more I got involved in the heritage field, the more it became clear to me that we are losing the sites and the stories faster than we can physically preserve them. Of course, earthquakes and all the natural phenomena—floods, tornadoes, etc.—take their toll. However, what occurred to me was human-caused destruction, which was not only causing a significant portion of the destruction, but actually it was accelerating. This includes arson, urban sprawl, acid rain, not to mention terrorism and wars. It was getting more and more apparent that we're fighting a losing battle. We're losing our sites and the stories, and basically we're losing a piece—and a significant piece—of our collective memory. Imagine us as a human race not knowing where we came from.

[. . .] Let me close with another short story. Two years ago, we were approached by a partner of ours to digitally preserve an important heritage site, a UNESCO heritage site in Uganda, the Royal Kasubi Tombs. The work was done successfully in the field, and the data was archived and publicly disseminated through the CyArk website. Last March, we received very sad news. The Royal Tombs had been destroyed by suspected arson. A few days later, we received a call: "Is the data available and can it be used for reconstruction?" Our answer, of course, was yes.

Let me leave you with a final thought. Our heritage is much more than our collective memory—it's our collective treasure. We owe it to our children, our grandchildren, and the generations we will never meet to keep it safe and to pass it along. Thank you.

This is an edited version of Kacyra's 2011 TED Talk. To watch the full talk, visit TED.com.

CAROLYN STEEL

How Food Shapes Our Cities

Part 1

How do you feed a city? It's one of the great questions of our time. Yet it's one that's rarely asked. We take it for granted that if we go into a shop or restaurant, or indeed into this theater's foyer in about an hour's time, there is going to be food there waiting for us, having magically come from somewhere.

But when you think that every day for a city the size of London, enough food has to be produced, transported, bought and sold, cooked, eaten, disposed of, and that something similar has to happen every day for every city on Earth, it's remarkable that cities get fed at all.

We live in places like this as if they're the most natural things in the world, forgetting that because we're animals and that we need to eat, we're actually as dependent on the natural world as our ancient ancestors were. And as more of us move into cities, more of that natural world is being transformed into extraordinary landscapes like the one behind me—it's soybean fields in Mato Grosso in Brazil—in order to feed us. These are extraordinary landscapes, but few of us ever get to see them.

And increasingly, these landscapes are not just feeding us either. As more of us move into cities, more of us are eating meat, so that a third of the annual grain crop globally now gets fed to animals rather than to us human animals. And given that it takes three times as much grain—actually ten times as much grain—to feed a human if it's passed through an animal first, that's not a very efficient way of feeding us.

And it's an escalating problem, too. By 2050, it's estimated that twice the number of us are going to be living in cities. And it's also estimated that there is going to be twice as much meat and dairy consumed. So meat and urbanism are rising hand in hand. And that's going to pose an enormous problem. Six billion hungry carnivores to feed, by 2050. That's a big problem. And actually if we carry on as we are, it's a problem we're very unlikely to be able to solve.

Nineteen million hectares of rain forest are lost every year to create new arable land. Although at the same time we're losing an equivalent amount of existing arables to salinization and erosion. We're very hungry for fossil fuels, too. It takes about 10 calories to produce every calorie of food that we consume in the West. And even though there is food that we are producing at great cost, we don't actually value it. Half the food produced in the U.S.A. is currently thrown away. And to end all of this, at the end of this long process, we're not even managing to feed the planet properly. A billion of us are obese, while a further billion starve. None of it makes very much sense.

And when you think that 80 percent of global trade in food now is controlled by just five multinational corporations, it's a grim picture. As we're moving into cities, the world is also embracing a Western diet. And if we look to the future, it's an unsustainable diet.

[. . .]

Part 2

Here we have food—that used to be the center, the social core of the city—at the periphery. It used to be a social event, buying and selling food. Now it's anonymous. We used to cook; now we just add water, or a little bit of an egg if you're making a cake or something. We don't smell food to see if it's OK to eat. We just read the back of a label on a packet. And we don't value food. We don't trust it. So instead of trusting it, we fear it. And instead of valuing it, we throw it away.

One of the great ironies of modern food systems is that they've made the very thing they promised to make easier much harder. By making it possible to build cities anywhere and any place, they've actually distanced us from our most important relationship, which is that of us and nature. And also they've made us dependent on systems that only they can deliver, that, as we've seen, are unsustainable.

So what are we going to do about that? It's not a new question. 500 years ago, it's what Thomas More was asking himself. This is the frontispiece of his book *Utopia*. And it was a series of semi-independent city-states, if that sounds remotely familiar, a day's walk from one another where everyone was basically farming-mad, and grew vegetables in their back gardens, and ate communal meals together, and so on. And I think you could argue that food is a fundamental ordering principle of Utopia, even though More never framed it that way.

[. . .] *Utopia* was actually a word that Thomas More used deliberately. It was a kind of joke, because it's got a double derivation from the Greek. It can either mean a good place, or no place. Because it's an ideal. It's an imaginary thing. We can't have it. And I think, as a conceptual tool for thinking about the very deep problem of human dwelling, that makes it not much use. So I've come up with an alternative, which is *Sitopia*, from the ancient Greek, "sitos" for food, and "topos" for place.

I believe we already live in Sitopia. We live in a world shaped by food, and if we realize that, we can use food as a really powerful tool—a conceptual tool, design tool, to shape the world differently. So if we were to do that, what might Sitopia look like? Well, I think it looks a bit like this. I have to use this slide. It's just the look on the face of the dog. But anyway, this is—it's food at the center of life, at the center of family life, being celebrated, being enjoyed, people taking time for it. This is where food should be in our society.

But you can't have scenes like this unless you have people like this. By the way, these can be men as well. It's people who think about food, who think ahead, who plan, who can stare at a pile of raw vegetables and actually recognize them. We need these people. They're part of a network. Because without these kinds of people, we can't have places like this. Here, I deliberately chose this because it is a man buying a vegetable. But networks, markets where food is being grown locally. It's common. It's fresh. It's part of the social life of the city. Because without that, you can't have this kind of place, food that is grown locally and also is part of the landscape, and is not just a zero-sum commodity off in some unseen hell-hole. Cows with a view. Steaming piles of humus. This is basically bringing the whole thing together.

And this is a community project I visited recently in Toronto. It's a greenhouse, where kids get told all about food and growing their own food. Here is a plant called Kevin, or maybe it's a plant belonging to a kid called Kevin. I don't know. But anyway, these kinds of projects that are trying to reconnect us with nature is extremely important.

So Sitopia, for me, is really a way of seeing. It's basically recognizing that Sitopia already exists in little pockets everywhere. The trick is to join them up, to use food as a way of seeing. And if we do that, we're going to stop seeing cities as big, metropolitan, unproductive blobs, like this. We're going to see them more like this, as part of the productive, organic framework of which they are inevitably a part, symbiotically connected. But of course, that's not a great image either, because we need not to be producing food like this anymore. We need to be thinking more about permaculture, which is why I think this image just sums up for me the kind of thinking we need to be doing. It's a re-conceptualization of the way food shapes our lives.

The best image I know of this is from 650 years ago. It's Ambrogio Lorenzetti's "Allegory of Good Government." It's about the relationship between the city and the countryside. And I think the message of this is very clear. If the city looks after the country, the country will look after the city. And I want us to ask now, what would Ambrogio Lorenzetti paint if he painted this image today? What would an allegory of good government look like today? Because I think it's an urgent question. It's one we have to ask and we have to start answering. We know we are what we eat. We need to realize that the world is also what we eat. But if we take that idea, we can use food as a really powerful tool to shape the world better. Thank you very much.

This is an edited version of Steel's 2009 TED Talk. To watch the full talk, visit TED.com.

Unit 8

ANDREW McAFEE
What Will Future Jobs Look Like?

Part 1

The writer George Eliot cautioned us that, among all forms of mistake, prophesy is the most gratuitous. The person that we would all acknowledge as her 20th-century counterpart, Yogi Berra, agreed. He said, "It's tough to make predictions, especially about the future."

I'm going to ignore their cautions and make one very specific forecast. In the world that we are creating very quickly, we're going to see more and more things that look like science fiction, and fewer and fewer things that look like jobs. Our cars are very quickly going to start driving themselves, which means we're going to need fewer truck drivers. We're going to hook Siri up to Watson and use that to automate a lot of the work that's currently done by customer service reps and troubleshooters and diagnosers, and we're already taking R2D2, painting him orange, and putting him to work carrying shelves around warehouses, which means we need a lot fewer people to be walking up and down those aisles.

Now, for about 200 years, people have been saying exactly what I'm telling you—the age of technological unemployment is at hand—starting with the Luddites smashing looms in Britain just about two centuries ago, and they have been wrong. Our economies in the developed world have coasted along on something pretty close to full employment.

Which brings up a critical question: Why is this time different, if it really is? The reason it's different is that, just in the past few years, our machines have started demonstrating skills they have never, ever had before: understanding, speaking, hearing, seeing, answering, writing, and they're still acquiring new skills. For example, mobile humanoid robots are still incredibly primitive, but the research arm of the Defense Department just launched a competition to have them do things like this, and if the track record is any guide, this competition is going to be successful. So when I look around, I think the day is not too far off at all when we're going to have androids doing a lot of the work that we are doing right now. And we're creating a world where there is going to be more and more technology and fewer and fewer jobs. It's a world that Erik Brynjolfsson and I are calling "the new machine age." The thing to keep in mind is that this is absolutely great news.

Part 2

[. . .] We are seeing an amazing flourishing taking place. In a world where it is just about as easy to generate an object as it is to print a document, we have amazing new possibilities.

The people who used to be craftsmen and hobbyists are now makers, and they're responsible for massive amounts of innovation. And artists who were formerly constrained can now do things that were never, ever possible for them before. So this is a time of great flourishing, and the more I look around, the more convinced I become that this quote, from the physicist Freeman Dyson, is not hyperbole at all. This is just a plain statement of the facts. We are in the middle of an astonishing period.

"Technology is a gift of God. After the gift of life it is perhaps the greatest of God's gifts. It is the mother of civilizations, of arts and of sciences." — Freeman Dyson

Which brings up another great question: What could possibly go wrong in this new machine age, right?

[. . .]

Part 3

To tell you the kinds of societal challenges that are going to come up in the new machine age, I want to tell a story about two stereotypical American workers. And to make them really stereotypical, let's make them both white guys. And the first one is a college-educated professional, creative type, manager, engineer, doctor, lawyer, that kind of worker. We're going to call him "Ted." He's at the top of the American middle class. His counterpart is not college-educated and works as a laborer, works as a clerk, does low-level white collar or blue collar work in the economy. We're going to call that guy "Bill."

And if you go back about 50 years, Bill and Ted were leading remarkably similar lives. For example, in 1960 they were both very likely to have full-time jobs, working at least 40 hours a week. But as the social researcher Charles Murray has documented, as we started to automate the economy, and 1960 is just about when computers started to be used by businesses, as we started to progressively inject technology and automation and digital stuff into the economy, the fortunes of Bill and Ted diverged a lot. Over this time frame, Ted has continued to hold a full-time job. Bill hasn't. In many cases, Bill has left the economy entirely, and Ted very rarely has. Over time, Ted's marriage has stayed quite happy. Bill's hasn't. And Ted's kids have grown up in a two-parent home, while Bill's absolutely have not over time. Other ways that Bill is dropping out of society? He's decreased his voting in presidential elections, and he's started to go to prison a lot more often. So I cannot tell a happy story about these social trends, and they don't show any signs of reversing themselves. They're also true no matter which ethnic group or demographic group we look at, and they're actually getting so severe that they're in danger of overwhelming even the amazing progress we made with the Civil Rights Movement.

And what my friends in Silicon Valley and Cambridge are overlooking is that they're Ted. They're living these amazingly busy, productive lives, and they've got all the benefits to show from that, while Bill is leading a very different life. They're actually both proof of how right Voltaire was when he talked about the benefits of work, and the fact that it saves us from not one but three great evils.

"Work saves a man from three great evils: boredom, vice, and need." — Voltaire

Part 4

[W]ith these challenges, what do we do about them?

The economic playbook is surprisingly clear, surprisingly straightforward, in the short term especially. The robots are not going to take all of our jobs in the next year or two, so the classic Econ 101 playbook is going to work just fine: Encourage entrepreneurship, double down on infrastructure, and make sure we're turning out people from our educational system with the appropriate skills.

But over the longer term, if we are moving into an economy that's heavy on technology and light on labor, and we are, then we have to consider some more radical interventions, for example, something like a guaranteed minimum income. [. . .] And if you find yourself worried that something like a guaranteed income is going to stifle our drive to succeed and make us kind of complacent, you might be interested to know that social mobility, one of the things we really pride ourselves on in the United States, is now lower than it is in the northern European countries that have these very generous social safety nets. So the economic playbook is actually pretty straightforward.

The societal one is a lot more challenging. I don't know what the playbook is for getting Bill to engage and stay engaged throughout life.

I do know that education is a huge part of it. I witnessed this firsthand. I was a Montessori kid for the first few years of my education, and what that education taught me is that the world is an interesting place and my job is to go explore it. The school stopped in third grade, so then I entered the public school system, and it felt like I had been sent to the Gulag. With the benefit of hindsight, I now know the job was to prepare me for life as a clerk or a laborer, but at the time it felt like the job was to kind of bore me into some submission with what was going on around me. We have to do better than this. We cannot keep turning out Bills.

[. . .] I started my talk with quotes from wordsmiths who were separated by an ocean and a century. Let me end it with words from politicians who were similarly distant.

Winston Churchill came to my home of MIT in 1949, and he said, "If we are to bring the broad masses of the people in every land to the table of abundance, it can only be by the tireless improvement of all of our means of technical production."

Abraham Lincoln realized there was one other ingredient. He said, "I am a firm believer in the people. If given the truth, they can be depended upon to meet any national crisis. The great point is to give them the plain facts."

So the optimistic note, great point that I want to leave you with is that the plain facts of the machine age are becoming clear, and I have every confidence that we're going to use them to chart a good course into the challenging, abundant economy that we're creating.

Thank you very much.

This is an edited version of McAfee's 2013 TED Talk. To watch the full talk, visit TED.com.

PATRICIA KUHL
The Linguistic Genius of Babies

Part 1

I want you to take a look at this baby. What you're drawn to are her eyes and the skin you love to touch. But today I'm going to talk to you about something you can't see—what's going on up in that little brain of hers. The modern tools of neuroscience are demonstrating to us that what's going on up there is nothing short of rocket science. And what we're learning is going to shed some light on what the romantic writers and poets described as the "celestial openness" of the child's mind.

[. . .] Work in my lab is focused on the first critical period in development—and that is the period in which babies try to master which sounds are used in their language. We think, by studying how the sounds are learned, we'll have a model for the rest of language, and perhaps for critical periods that may exist in childhood for social, emotional, and cognitive development. So we've been studying the babies using a technique that we're using all over the world and the sounds of all languages. The baby sits on a parent's lap, and we train them to turn their heads when a sound changes—like from "ah" to "ee." If they do so at the appropriate time, the black box lights up and a panda bear pounds a drum. A six-monther adores the task.

What have we learned? Well, babies all over the world are what I like to describe as "citizens of the world." They can discriminate all the sounds of all languages, no matter what country we're testing and what language we're using, and that's remarkable because you and I can't do that. We're culture-bound listeners. We can discriminate the sounds of our own language, but not those of foreign languages. So the question arises: When do those citizens of the world turn into the language-bound listeners that we are? And the answer: before their first birthdays. What you see here is performance on that head-turn task for babies tested in Tokyo and the United States, here in Seattle, as they listened to "ra" and "la"—sounds important to English, but not to Japanese. So at six to eight months, the babies are totally equivalent. Two months later, something incredible occurs. The babies in the United States are getting a lot better, babies in Japan are getting a lot worse, but both of those groups of babies are preparing for exactly the language that they are going to learn.

So the question is: What's happening during this critical two-month period? This is the critical period for sound development, but what's going on up there? So there are two things going on. The first is that the babies are listening intently to us, and they're taking statistics as they listen to us talk—they're taking statistics. So listen to two mothers speaking motherese—the universal language we use when we talk to kids—first in English and then in Japanese.

[Video] *English Mother: Ah, I love your big blue eyes—so pretty and nice.*

Japanese Mother: [Japanese]

Part 2

During the production of speech, when babies listen, what they're doing is taking statistics on the language that they hear. And those distributions grow. And what we've learned is that babies are sensitive to the statistics, and the statistics of Japanese and English are very, very different. English has a lot of Rs and Ls. The distribution shows. And the distribution of Japanese is totally different, where we see a group of intermediate sounds, which is known as the Japanese "R." So babies absorb the statistics of the language and it changes their brains; it changes them from the citizens of the world to the culture-bound listeners that we are. But we as adults are no longer absorbing those statistics. We're governed by the representations in memory that were formed early in development.

So what we're seeing here is changing our models of what the critical period is about. We're arguing from a mathematical standpoint that the learning of language material may slow down when our distributions stabilize. It's raising lots of questions about bilingual people. Bilinguals must keep two sets of statistics in mind at once and flip between them, one after the other, depending on who they're speaking to.

[. . .] We want to get inside the brain and see this thing happening as babies are in front of televisions, as opposed to in front of human beings. Thankfully, we have a new machine, magnetoencephalography, that allows us to do this. It looks like a hair dryer from Mars. But it's completely safe, completely noninvasive, and silent. We're looking at millimeter accuracy with regard to spatial and millisecond accuracy using 306 SQUIDs—these are Superconducting QUantum Interference Devices—to pick up the magnetic fields that change as we do our thinking. We're the first in the world to record babies in an MEG machine while they are learning.

So this is little Emma. She's a six-monther. And she's listening to various languages in the earphones that are in her ears. You can see, she can move around. We're tracking her head with little pellets in a cap, so she's free to move completely unconstrained. It's a technical tour de force. What are we seeing? We're seeing the baby brain. As the baby hears a word in her language, the auditory areas light up, and then subsequently areas surrounding it that we think are related to coherence, getting the brain coordinated with its different areas, and causality, one brain area causing another to activate.

We are embarking on a grand and golden age of knowledge about child's brain development. We're going to be able to see a child's brain as they experience an emotion, as they learn to speak and read, as they solve a math problem, as they have an idea. And we're going to be able to invent brain-based interventions for children who have difficulty learning. Just as the poets and writers described, we're going to be able to see, I think, that wondrous openness, utter and complete openness, of the mind of a child. In investigating the child's brain, we're going to uncover deep truths about what it means to be human, and in the process, we may be able to help keep our own minds open to learning for our entire lives.

This is an edited version of Kuhl's 2011 TED Talk. To watch the full talk, visit TED.com.

Unit 10

BILL GATES
Innovating to Zero!

Part 1

I'm going to talk today about energy and climate. And that might seem a bit surprising because my full-time work at the Foundation is mostly about vaccines and seeds, about the things that we need to invent and deliver to help the poorest two billion live better lives. But energy and climate are extremely important to these people—in fact, more important than to anyone else on the planet. The climate getting worse means that many years, their crops won't grow; There will be too much rain, not enough rain, things will change in ways that their fragile environment simply can't support. And that leads to starvation, it leads to uncertainty, it leads to unrest. So, the climate changes will be terrible for them.

Also, the price of energy is very important to them. In fact, if you could pick just one thing to lower the price of, to reduce poverty, by far you would pick energy. Now, the price of energy has come down over time. Really advanced civilization is based on advances in energy. The coal revolution fueled the Industrial Revolution, and, even in the 1900s we've seen a very rapid decline in the price of electricity, and that's why we have refrigerators, air-conditioning, we can make modern materials and do so many things. And so, we're in a wonderful situation with electricity in the rich world. But, as we make it cheaper—and let's go for making it twice as cheap—we need to meet a new constraint, and that constraint has to do with CO_2.

CO_2 is warming the planet, and the equation on CO_2 is actually a very straightforward one. If you sum up the CO_2 that gets emitted, that leads to a temperature increase, and that temperature increase leads to some very negative effects: the effects on the weather; perhaps worse, the indirect effects, in that the natural ecosystems can't adjust to these rapid changes, and so you get ecosystem collapses.

Now, the exact amount of how you map from a certain increase of CO_2 to what temperature will be and where the positive feedbacks are, there's some uncertainty there, but not very much. And there's certainly uncertainty about how bad those effects will be, but they will be extremely bad. I asked the top scientists on this several times: Do we really have to get down to near zero? Can't we just cut it in half or a quarter? And the answer is that until we get near to zero, the temperature will continue to rise. And so that's a big challenge. It's very different than saying "We're a twelve-foot-high truck trying to get under a ten-foot bridge, and we can just sort of squeeze under." This is something that has to get to zero.

Now, we put out a lot of carbon dioxide every year, over 26 billion tons. For each American, it's about 20 tons; for people in poor countries, it's less than one ton. It's an average of about five tons for everyone on the planet. And, somehow, we have to make changes that will bring that down to zero. It's been constantly going up. It's only various economic changes that have even flattened it at all, so we have to go from rapidly rising to falling, and falling all the way to zero.

Part 2

This equation has four factors, a little bit of multiplication: So, you've got a thing on the left, CO_2, that you want to get to zero, and that's going to be based on the number of people, the services each person's using on average, the energy on average for each service, and the CO_2 being put out per unit of energy. So let's look at each one of these and see how we can get this down to zero. Probably, one of these numbers is going to have to get pretty near to zero. Now that's back from high school algebra, but let's take a look.

First, we've got population. The world today has 6.8 billion people. That's headed up to about nine billion. Now, if we do a really great job on new vaccines, health care, reproductive health services, we could lower that by, perhaps, 10 or 15 percent, but there we see an increase of about 1.3.

The second factor is the services we use. This encompasses everything: the food we eat, clothing, TV, heating. These are very good things; Getting rid of poverty means providing these services to almost everyone on the planet. And it's a great thing for this number to go up. In the rich world, perhaps the top one billion, we probably could cut back and use less, but every year, this number, on average, is going to go up, and so, overall, that will more than double the services delivered per person. Here we have a very basic service: Do you have lighting in your house to be able to read your homework? And, in fact, these kids don't, so they're going out and reading their schoolwork under the street lamps.

Now, efficiency, E, the energy for each service, here finally we have some good news. We have something that's not going up. Through various inventions and new ways of doing lighting, through different types of cars, different ways of building buildings—there are a lot of services where you can bring the energy for that service down quite substantially. Some individual services even bring it down by 90 percent. There are other services like how we make fertilizer, or how we do air transport, where the rooms for improvement are far, far less. And so, overall here, if we're optimistic, we may get a reduction of a factor of three to even, perhaps, a factor of six. But for these first three factors now, we've gone from 26 billion to, at best, maybe 13 billion tons, and that just won't cut it.

So let's look at this fourth factor—this is going to be a key one—and this is the amount of CO_2 put out per each unit of energy. And so the question is: Can you actually get that to zero? If you burn coal, no. If you burn natural gas, no. Almost every way we make electricity today, except for the emerging renewables and nuclear, puts out CO_2. And so, what we're going to have to do at a global scale, is create a new system. And so, we need energy miracles.

Now, when I use the term "miracle," I don't mean something that's impossible. The microprocessor is a miracle. The personal computer is a miracle. The Internet and its services are a miracle. So the people here have participated in the creation of many miracles. Usually, we don't have a deadline, where you have to get the miracle by a certain date. Usually, you just kind of stand by, and some come along, some don't. This is a case where we actually have to drive at full speed and get a miracle in a pretty tight timeline.

Part 3

[. . .] So let's think: How should we measure ourselves? What should our report card look like? Well, let's go out to where we really need to get, and then look at the intermediate. For 2050, you've heard many people talk about this 80 percent reduction. That really is very important, that we get there. And that 20 percent will be used up by things going on in poor countries, still some agriculture, hopefully we will have cleaned up forestry, cement. So to get to that 80 percent, the developed countries, including countries like China, will have had to switch their electricity generation altogether. So, the other grade is: Are we deploying this zero-emission technology, have we deployed it in all the developed countries and we're in the process of getting it elsewhere? That's super important. That's a key element of making that report card.

So, backing up from there, what should the 2020 report card look like? Well, again, it should have the two elements. We should go through these efficiency measures to start getting reductions: The less we emit, the less that sum will be of CO_2, and, therefore, the less the temperature. But in some ways, the grade we get there, doing things that don't get us all the way to the big reductions, is only equally, or maybe even slightly less, important than the other, which is the pace of innovation on these breakthroughs.

[. . .] So this is a wish. It's a very concrete wish that we invent this technology. If you gave me only one wish for the next 50 years—I could pick who's president, I could pick a vaccine, which is something I love, or I could pick that this thing that's half the cost with no CO_2 gets invented—this is the wish I would pick. This is the one with the greatest impact. If we don't get this wish, the division between the people who think short term and long term will be terrible, between the U.S. and China, between poor countries and rich, and most of all the lives of those two billion will be far worse.

So what do we have to do? What am I appealing to you to step forward and drive? We need to go for more research funding. When countries get together in places like Copenhagen, they shouldn't just discuss the CO_2. They should discuss this innovation agenda, and you'd be stunned at the ridiculously low levels of spending on these innovative approaches. We do need the market incentives—CO_2 tax, cap and trade—something that gets that price signal out there. We need to get the message out. We need to have this dialogue be a more rational, more understandable dialogue, including the steps that the government takes. This is an important wish, but it is one I think we can achieve.

This is an edited version of Gates's 2010 TED Talk. To watch the full talk, visit TED.com.

VOCABULARY LOG

As you complete each unit, use this chart to record definitions and example sentences of key vocabulary. Add other useful words or phrases you learn.

Unit	Vocabulary	Definition/Example
1	acquire*	
	authority*	
	consult*	
	encounter*	
	innately	
	obsessed (with)	
	prospect*	
	solely*	
	variant*	
	visionary*	
	_____	
2	constraint*	
	contagious	
	enthusiasm	
	facility	
	guarantee*	
	input*	
	let go of	
	mentor	
	prescribe	
	security*	
	_____	
3	aspire	
	collaboration	
	donate	
	endorse	
	found*	
	fulfill	
	mirror	
	stereotype	
	take on	
	volunteer*	
	_____	
4	analyze*	
	dimension*	
	distinct*	
	genre	
	highlight*	
	identical*	
	obviously*	
	option*	
	proficiency	
	societal	
	_____	

Unit	Vocabulary	Definition/Example
5	access*	
	circumstance*	
	compassion	
	eradicate	
	goodwill	
	implication*	
	intimate	
	overwhelmed	
	struggle	
	unexpected	
	_____	
6	deteriorate	
	heritage	
	incorporate*	
	intensity*	
	occur*	
	preserve	
	sacred	
	site*	
	symbolic*	
	thereby*	
	_____	
7	accelerate	
	dilemma	
	emit	
	inefficient	
	pose*	
	precise*	
	prosper	
	simultaneously	
	unreliable*	
	yield	
	_____	

Unit	Vocabulary	Definition/Example
8	capability*	
	deduce*	
	mission	
	niche	
	novel	
	obsolete	
	retain*	
	routine	
	theme*	
	unconventional*	
	_____	
9	abuse	
	accustomed to	
	ban	
	barrier	
	discriminate*	
	downside	
	eliminate*	
	initially*	
	instinctive	
	justify*	
	_____	
10	alternative*	
	concentrated*	
	diminishing*	
	dramatically*	
	emerging*	
	equivalent*	
	ingenuity	
	intrinsic*	
	require*	
	transition*	
	_____	

* These words are on the Academic Word List (AWL), a list of the 570 most frequent word families in academic texts. The AWL does not include words that are among the most frequent 2,000 words of English. For more information, see www.victoria.ac.nz/lals/resources/academicwordlist/

Text Credits

10–13 Adapted from "The Restless Gene," by David Dobbs: NGM January 2013, **26–29** Adapted from "Musings of a male granny: This retired schoolteacher spends his free time Skyping with Indian schoolkids," by Natasha Scripture: http://blog.ted.com October 14 2014, **42–45** Adapted from "Teen entrepreneur Avani Singh: `You can make a difference,'" by Liz Jacobs: http://ideas.ted.com December 6 2013, **58–61** Adapted from "A science fiction and fantasy reading list for teen creativity," by Laura McClure: http://ideas.ted.com June 20 2014, **74–77** Adapted from "Q&A: Renée C. Byer's Living on a Dollar a Day," by Becky Harlan: NG online April 15 2014, **90–93** Adapted from "Backing Up History," by Elizabeth Preston: NGM October 2010, and "Laser Archaeology," by George Johnson: NGM December 2013, **106–108** Adapted from "Feeding the World," by Jonathon Foley: NGM May 2015, **122–125** Adapted from "Can a Computer Cook?" by Rebecca Rupp: NG online June 19 2014, **138–141** Adapted from "Babies can tell apart different languages with visual clues alone," by Ed Yong: NG online March 7 2009, and "Five-month-old babies prefer their own languages and shun foreign accents," by Ed Yong: NG online June 14 2009, **154–157** Adapted from "Paths to the Future," by Bill McKibben: NGM March 2009.

NGM = National Geographic Magazine

Photo Credits

8–9 ©NASA/JPL-Caltech; **10–11**(tr) ©STEPHEN ALVAREZ/National Geographic Creative; **12**(t) ©John T. Burgoyne/National Geographic Creative; **13**(b) ©RICH REID/National Geographic Creative; **15** ©NASA/JPL-Caltech/MSSS; **17**(br) ©Fine Art/Corbis; **18–19**(t) ©Robert Leslie/TED; **20**(b) ©NASA/JPL/SSI; **21**(br) ©Science Photo Library/Science Photo Library/Corbis; **23**(t) ©NASA; **24–25** ©Joshua Lott/The New York Times/Redux; **26–27**(t) ©Nishant Shukla/Made by Many; **29**(b) ©School in the Cloud; **33**(b) ©Jerry Rothwell; **35** ©TED; **39**(t) ©Angelika Warmuth/Corbis Wire/Corbis; **40–41** ©Peter Essick/Aurora Photos; **42–43**(tr) AMI VITALE/National Geographic Creative; **44**(tl) ©IANS; **46**(t) ©Jorge Silva/Reuters; **47**(tc) ©AP Images/Tsering Topgyal; **50–51**(tr) ©James Duncan Davidson/TED; **55**(t) ©Denis Balibouse/Reuters; **56–57** ©Paramount/Bad Robot/The Kobal Collection/Picture Desk; **58–59** ©Michael Whelan; **60**(b) ©Ognen Teofilovski/Reuters; **61**(tr) ©Goodreads; (bl) ©Goodreads; **64**(b) ©Roland Shainidze Photography/Getty Images; **66–67**(tr) © Robert Leslie/TED; **71**(t) ©AF Archive/Alamy; **72–73** ©Renée Byer; **74–75**(tr) ©2011 John Grimwade Information Graphics/National Geographic Creative; **77**(t) ©Renée Byer; **78**(t) ©Renée Byer; **82–83**(tr) ©James Duncan Davidson /TED; **85**(t) ©ONE Foundation; **87**(t) ©Annie Griffiths/National Geographic Creative; **88–89** ©DAVID COVENTRY/National Geographic Creative; **90–91**(tl) ©skybucket3d.com, (tr) ©Ariadne Van Zandbergen/Getty Images; **92**(t) ©David Moir/Reuters; **93** ©NGM Staff/National Geographic Creative; **94**(b) ©Liu Liqun/Nomad/Corbis; **99** ©TED FLICKR; **101**(b) ©DEA/G. DAGLI ORTI/De Agostini/Getty Images; **103**(tl) ©Reuters/Corbis; (tr) ©Reuters/Corbis; **104–105** ©Paulo Fridman/Corbis; **106–107**(tl) ©JIM RICHARDSON/National Geographic Creative; (tc) ©JIM RICHARDSON/National Geographic Creative; (tr) ©JIM RICHARDSON/National Geographic Creative; **114–115**(tr) ©James Duncan Davidson/TED; **119**(t) ©Vince Talotta/Getty Images; **120–121** ©Beth Hall/Bloomberg/Getty Images; **122–123**(tr) ©JOHANNES EISELE/Getty Images; **124**(t) ©Jack Plunkett Feature Photo Service/Newscom; **125**(b) ©PAULO WHITAKER/Reuters/Corbis; **126**(t) ©Seth Wenig/AP Images; **130–131**(tr) ©James Duncan Davidson/TED; **135**(t) © Gaetan Bally/KEYSTONE/Redux; **136–137** © LYNN JOHNSON/National Geographic Creative; **138–139**(t) ©LYNN JOHNSON/National Geographic Creative; **141**(bl) ©Happy Art/Shutterstock.com **145**(b) ©LYNN JOHNSON/National Geographic Creative; **147** ©Patricia Kuhl/TED; **151**(t) ©Kike Calvo/National Geographic Creative; **152–153** ©YASUYOSHI CHIBA/Getty Images; **154–155**(tr) ©Stefan Kiefer/Canopy/Corbis; (bl) ©MARK THIESSEN/National Geographic Creative; **156–157**(tr) ©Skip Brown/National Geographic Images; **159** ©Tyrone Turner/National Geographic Creative; **163**(b) ©Peerakit JIrachetthakun/Getty Images; **164–165** ©James Duncan Davidson/TED; **167**(tl) ©Steve Debenport/Getty Images; (tl) ©Alex Studio/Shutterstock.com; (tr) ©Somchai Som/Shutterstock.com; (tr) ©Mavrick/Shutterstock.com; **169**(t) ©Ty Milford/Aurora Photos.

Illustrations:

45(c) Source: ILO, EAPEP, 6th edition; **109**(tr) Virginia W. Mason and Jason Treat, NGM Staff; Sources: Roger Hooke, University of Maine; David Tilman, University of Minnesota; **140**(t) Graphic: Lawson Parker; Sources: Charles Nelson, Harvard Medical School; Pat Levitt, Children's Hospital Los Angeles. Synapse Drawings based on Golgi Stain Preparations (1939–1967) by J L Conel; **158–159** Sean McNaughton, NG Staff; Source: McKinsey and Company.

Acknowledgements

The Authors and Publisher would like to thank the following teaching professionals for their valuable input during the development of this series:

Coleeta Paradise Abdullah, Certified Training Center; **Wilder Yesid Escobar Almeciga,** Universidad El Bosque; **Tara Amelia Arntsen,** Northern State University; **Mei-ho Chiu,** Soochow University; **Amy Cook,** Bowling Green State University; **Anthony Sean D'Amico,** SDH Institute; **Mariel Doyenart,** Alianza Cultural Uruguay-Estados Unidos; **Raichle Farrelly,** American University of Armenia; **Douglas E. Forster,** Japan Women's University; **Rosario Giraldez,** Alianza Cultural Uruguay Estados Unidos; **Floyd H. Graham III,** Kansai Gaidai University; **Jay Klaphake,** Kyoto University of Foreign Studies; **Anthony G. Lavigne,** Kansai Gaidai University; **Adriana Castañeda Londoño,** Centro Colombo Americano; **Alexandra Dylan Lowe,** SUNY Westchester Community College; **Elizabeth Ortiz Lozada,** COPEI–COPOL English Institute; **David Matijasevich,** Canadian Education College; **Jennie Popp,** Universidad Andrés Bello; **Ubon Pun-ubon,** Sripatum University; **Yoko Sakurai,** Aichi University; **Michael J. Sexton,** PSB Academy; **Jenay Seymour,** Hongik University; **Karenne Sylvester,** New College Manchester; **Mark S. Turnoy;** **Hajime Uematsu,** Hirosaki University; **Nae-Dong Yang,** National Taiwan University;

And special thanks to: Mary Kadera, Michael Whelan, Renee Byer, ONE Foundation, SkyBucket 3d and The School in the Cloud